1

This book is dedicated to my mom ᴖ
me and they never gave up.

Names of people have been changed.

Foreword

As a young mother of three in the 1980's - 90's, I often heard the saying, *You are never as happy as your unhappiest child.* My belief in that mantra almost robbed me of a decade of my life. After all, how could I be happy about anything if I had a child who was clearly struggling with something serious. Regardless of the fact that two of my three children were following the normal course of life... college, first jobs, marriage... my worries about David led to night after night of sleeplessness. *Where is David? Why did another job, another roommate, another relationship, another _____ not work out? Why do his eyes look funny? Is he hiding something in that backpack? Why isn't he returning my phone calls and texts? Why does he hide out upstairs? Does he need help? What kind of help? Why won't he talk to me?* Night after night of unanswered questions. And it wasn't until I read the book you currently have in your hands that many of these questions were answered.

This may surprise you. After all, David lived in the small upstairs attic bedroom of our home on and off during the last several years at the height of his alcoholism and addiction. Yet, it is amazing what can be hidden by a functional addict. David always had a plausible reason why his latest roommate had not worked out or why he had quit his most recent job. As his mom, I wanted to believe him, so I chose to do so. In many ways, David was living here yet was *not* living here. I would see him for a few minutes in the early morning when he would join me in our front room where I sat in what I called my "devotional chair," praying and searching mightily for answers in scripture. Those few minutes of connection gave me a glimpse of the David I raised... my quiet and introspective middle child....my artistic son who created beautiful artwork and whose homemade movies made our family laugh until we cried...my child who would back away from any conflict and always strived to please throughout elementary, middle, and high school. This was the David I saw before me for a few minutes each morning. Then, he would be off, and I often did not see him again until the next morning. After reading his book, I learned what his days and nights were truly like.

When David moved to Nashville, we tried hard to give him a fresh start and all of the support he needed through various counselors and organizations. Over the next several years, there were many periods when we truly believed he had conquered his demons because, from the outside, things seemed to be going well for him. Yet, the devil of addiction was always lurking around the corner, and suddenly things would be "a bit off" with David– soon to be followed by another crisis. I know people will ask, "If you knew, or even suspected, he was having issues with alcoholism and drug addiction, why did you let him move back in each time? Weren't you enabling his behavior?" Maybe we were. But, as parents, you want so badly to believe in your child. When money went missing from our home, we chose to believe David when he claimed he hadn't taken it. When some leftover prescription pain medicine was no longer in the cabinet, we questioned our own memory about its whereabouts after David vehemently denied taking it. These types of incidents happened over the course of months and years, and a parent's memory of wrongs can be very short.

One lesson I have learned through this experience is there is not one course of action for recovery. What works for one person and situation may not work at all for another. Some parents get to the point where they have to shut their door for a final time, and many young adults will say it was at this point they finally turned around and sought help. Honestly, we were very close to reaching that crossroads. Yet, during David's final spiraling months, we saw a scared, lonely stranger living in our beloved son's body, and we wanted him to know we were there for him unconditionally. Eventually, I think that is why David came home after checking himself out of rehab. He knew we wouldn't turn him away.

I needed my own help to survive through all of this, and I found it in a parent Al-Anon group. During those meetings, I learned I was not alone. When you have a child who gets lost in the world of alcoholism and addiction, you grow very reflective. You wonder, *How did this happen? What could I have done differently? What did I do wrong?* There tends to be a very short road to blame, and while it should sit squarely on the shoulders of the alcoholic or addict, I too easily blamed myself. It's hard not to when you see the young adult children of your friends thriving along the highway of normal adulthood. Although I had two such children myself, I would grow very quiet when speaking about them because I knew someone would inevitably ask, "Well, how is David doing?" David chose his title *Pretty Quiet* as it reflects on his own personality and how it describes the quiet, yet deadly, way addiction creeps into a person's life. I think *Pretty Quiet* can also describe a parent's journey…. quiet on the outside, yet screaming in anguish on the inside.

Codependency is not a word I had ever heard before I read Melanie Beatty's book *Codependent No More,* yet I quickly saw myself in its pages. I learned through reading that book, and other Al-Anon literature, that I had to focus on my own well-being if I was going to survive this. I learned it was good and right for me to choose happiness, regardless of the unknowns happening in David's life. However, on December 24, 2020, when David did not show up for Christmas Eve dinner nor could we reach him on Christmas morning, it was hard to focus on anything other than praying David was alive.

My faith in God's power to redeem David was tested many times, yet I found solace in Christ's promise that He was with David even when I had no clue where he was or what he was doing. Like the Alcoholics Anonymous 12 Steps, Al-Anon's are very similar and Step 3 particularly resonated with me. It speaks of turning your will and your life over to the care of God as you understand him. Daily, I turned my life *and* David's life over to God as I reminded myself that I had no control over his choices. Frankly, I don't know how you cope with alcoholism and addiction without faith. One Saturday when things were unraveling, my daughter Mattie and I decided to get *Faith* tattoos as a reminder to never give up hope. As Hebrews 11:1 states, *Faith is confidence in what we hope for and assurance about what we do not see.* At the time, I wanted so badly to *see* David thriving and moving forward in his life, free from drugs and alcohol. I look at my tattoo now, and I praise God for where David is in his journey.

David wrote this book during his first year in recovery. He told me he wanted to show how a "normal person with a happy, normal childhood" can get so easily lost and entrapped in a very dark world. He hopes the book will help loved ones understand the thinking of someone addicted to drugs and alcohol. Most importantly, David wants to make clear that the person you love is still there and is capable of finding freedom and wholeness again. David would be the first to say to someone striving for recovery, *"If I can do it, you can too."*

David's journey was hard for me to read. I questioned him many times, *"Are you sure you want to put all of this out there? Some people may look at you differently or judge you by your past,"* and for those of you who know me personally, you won't be surprised to hear that I asked, *"Won't you at least change some of your language?"* However, David wants people to know his whole story. As he replied to me, *"No more hiding, no more shame, no more lies."* It takes courage to bring your secrets into the light. It takes accepting forgiveness from God, from loved ones, and ultimately forgiving yourself as you embark on a new course.

I could not be more proud of my courageous and strong son.

David, I love you,

Mom

Martha Newson
August 5, 2022

Pretty Quiet

David Newson

1

Beginnings End

2018 had ended abruptly, or so I thought. I sat in my parents' attic in Nashville, Tennessee, a broken boy at twenty-eight, thinking about what I had done. It was hard to remember every little detail through the bottles of alcohol, thick marijuana smoke, and the cocktail of drugs I was consuming on a daily basis. I had taken too many wrong turns to make it back. I was a boy who missed the bus to adulthood. I was full of shame, regret, and whatever other self-deprecating emotion I could fill my mind with. The depression, alcoholism, and drug abuse I never addressed was finally coming full circle. I had heard the horror stories of such things growing up but naively thought it couldn't happen to me. But there I was, grappling in the wake of addiction. Addiction had come at me slowly. Little did I know, things would get much worse.

My parents did everything they could to set me up for success, yet I still failed. I thought I checked all the boxes; graduating college, working a decent job, getting engaged. Life had seemingly given me everything on a silver platter, but I gradually lost it all. It was a slow trickle of bad decisions that eventually burst. And it was my decisions alone that left me behind.

I sat there in a thick haze wondering what to do next. The large quantities of drugs and alcohol from the previous week still hadn't cleared and the fact that my engagement was called off still wasn't registering. It would take time to heal. It would take rehab, therapy, and the 12-step program to get me out of this shit situation. It would take something greater than myself. They were all logical and healthy directions to steer this broken vessel, but with a drunk captain, the right direction was clear to everyone but myself.

The wedding was supposed to be in three weeks. It would be three long weeks of sad anticipation. Nothing had panned out the way I thought it would, but I shouldn't have been surprised—it was all my fault. It was me. I was at that point because of my choices. I was at that point because my addiction was in charge. I was stuck in time, space or whatever you want to call it. Stuck in the upstairs room at my parents' house in Nashville. I still wasn't sure what to do, but I was tired of being "pretty quiet."

I was a quiet kid who straddled the line between shy and outgoing. I was a kid who valued his friends and his alone time equally. I could start on the recreational basketball team in the morning, then spend the whole afternoon alone drawing. I was a kid with multiple interests that changed based on the month and the season. Like most kids, I was curious about what made the world tick.

My family traveled when I was a kid. We went to Edisto Island for the holidays and out west on vacation. I had walked the streets of Las Vegas, enamored with the lights that never turned off and rode the roller coaster on the Santa Monica pier at sunset. I hiked to the top of Grandfather Mountain and stood at the edge of the Grand Canyon. The world seemed so large, yet so attainable. There was no line that couldn't be crossed. I believed anything was possible. It was that childhood wonder that would fade as I got older. It was the realization that in the shadows of the neon lights was addiction and hopelessness. And the golden desert reflection of the Mirage Hotel would soon fade with the rising tide of chemical dependence.

I was born into a family of five; an older brother named Drew and a little sister named Mattie. I, of course, was the middle child and that comes with its own set of preconceived problems. All three of us were different in our own right.

Being the second-born made it easier to fly under the radar for most of my life. It was always my older brother, Drew, who took the heat growing up. But at that moment in late 2018, the truth of my life was in full focus and all eyes were on me.

The nineties had been a different time where life seemed simple. I remember the hill on Braeburn Road. It was big and brushed the start of the sky. It had a long, steady slant that ran through a series of brick houses on the left and right. On one snowy day in 1995, I was standing at the bottom of its icy veins, piercing my eyes on the snow-covered oak trees that lined its gutter. I had been up and down the hill many times before and was about to give it one last go on my sled.

The road was full of potholes in various shades of gray, creating organic shapes throughout its entirety. From the mundane cyclic parts of life to childhood memories, Braeburn Road sourced them all. The road wound through the Stonehaven maze, and at the base of the hill was a one-story ranch house. It was the house I was born into. In the backyard was a play set with a yellow and red swing and a small concrete patio where fireflies would pulse with their red and orange glow.

It was freezing on that late March day and an unusual cold spell had cast a grip over Charlotte. The purple and red tones on my skin traveled from my tiny toes, up through my ankles and legs. The city had been shut down for days and school was out. The busy roads were clear and a soft, white blanket of untouched snow glittered like diamonds. Charlotte never got much more than a dusting so this was unusual and special. Luckily, we still had power.

My winter clothes never fit. From my teal-blue Hornets cap to the two-toned brown driving gloves and the extra-large Carolina Panthers socks, the winter bin was full of surprises. It had years and years of hand-me-downs and almost everything was oversized. I didn't care, though. The snow was melting and I wasn't stopping. That type of fun only came once a year at best. The gray of the day and soft pink cast by the nearby city buildings at night would run upside down. By that point, I had been outside for days playing with neighborhood friends.

I started walking up the hill for one last go on the Red Flyer my parents pulled from the attic, its steel red beams full of scuff marks. Pulled with a thin white string, it weighed more than my little arms could handle. I slid a time or two but eventually made it to the top. The hill was crowded that day; people scattered about wearing brightly colored jackets and parents were on accident prevention duty trying to stop their precious children from running into parked cars. I felt big looking down the hill. I was an adolescent with adult eyes. Who knew where my parents were? They let me explore the neighborhood on my own and weren't overly doting. I loved them and they loved me, loved me enough to let me find adventure.

I knew every nook of the neighborhood, every cranny for 'kick the can' and each house that gave out the best candy during Halloween. I knew the longest run for the fastest bike speeds and every shortcut to the nearest gas station. I loved buying Lemonheads, Gobstoppers, Zebra Gum and Cheerwine there with the few dollars my parents would give me. I would wander back off the main road and eat my treats under the bridge on Monroe Road, away from the hot summer sun. The McAlpine Greenway was attached at the corner of the neighborhood. The path sloped downwards into the woods where there was a creek that would often flood. I'd try and forge it right after a storm. Sometimes I could get across.

I squared up my Flyer and readied it for departure. I whipped past blurry faces and broken-down tree limbs, my face full of tortured excitement. It felt good going fast. It felt good feeling out of control. It was a feeling that would stay with me for twenty-five more years, living off chaos and self destruction.

I swerved to avoid a few people and planted my Reeboks on the ground. My Flyer spun around left, throwing me off onto the black ice that was so well crushed before me. A few scrapes never hurt anyone, but eventually they'd take a toll.

In the summer I'd ride my bike to Rama Swim Club. It was in the neighborhood and most families were members. There was a shortcut through a small patch of bushes at the end of a cul-de-sac a half mile from home. Opening day was always a huge deal, and I spent most of my summer days there. The concession stand might have been the best part. On those hot, humid, summer days, I sipped on slowly melting Rocket Pops and guzzled down giant Pixie Sticks.

I'd play with all sorts of water toys. I had a red boat that glided over the water and weighted colorful rings that I'd fetch from the bottom of the pool. My friends and I would fight each other with giant foam pool sticks and climb each other's backs to chicken fight; being as tall as I was, I was always the base. We'd play Marco Polo and set imaginary boundaries, so the game wouldn't last forever. I'd eat Pizza Hut by the pool and stub my big toe on the concrete running towards the water.

Adult swim always sucked. I'd wait by the side of the pool with my feet in the water, watching the three people who joined the wrinkle society floating around like burlap sacks in salt water. It usually lasted thirty minutes, yet it felt like the sound of the lifeguard's whistle took forever. When it finally blew, every kid jumped in, creating a massive wave that boiled over the edge.

I could never touch the deep end during sharks and minnows. It was twelve feet deep and the pressure always got to me by eight. Reaching the bottom was the only free pass to the other side. Older kids were ruthless, and it taught me to act tough, even though I really wasn't. My older brother, Drew, was a good teacher in the game of growth. We'd butt heads and he'd pick on me constantly.

Drew is two and a half years older than me, but it always felt like he was older than that. He's taller than me, being six foot, six inches tall, and I looked up to him, literally. He was an athletic kid who played basketball and had a big circle of friends. His hair had that southern boy flip, and he liked to watch professional wrestling on television. Drew was a kid who was always getting into trouble at school and had a rebellious side to him. He'd flirt with girls and wear a tie with a golf shirt on game day just to piss off the coach. He'd flood the physical education locker room for no reason and skip out on doing half his homework. Drew was the cool kid, and I wanted to be like him. He was tough on me growing up, like any other older brother would be.

One time, he and his buddy put two screws in some plywood attached to a ragtag piece of firewood. It was their best attempt at a bike ramp, and they asked me to give it a test run. I wanted to impress him. I loved my brother. But a broken arm later and a bowl of disappointment didn't fix my growing pains.

There was a long hallway that led to my parents' bedroom on the left, and my brother and I shared a bedroom on the right. Our window faced the street and I vividly remember watching people with their dogs walk by. We had bunk beds and a trundle bed that pulled out from the bottom when friends came over. I'd build forts out of sheets, held up with tacks and the tips of brooms, and fill the inside with pillows and Christmas lights. Fort building felt like I could control my own space. It was a place I could create that was completely my own. I did it alone and felt like an escape from my older brother and the outside world. I customized it with pictures of Britney Spears and Limp Bizkit, which were taped to the horizontal wooden beams.

We moved to a cul-de-sac when I was six, Kenyon Court to be exact, to a house about a mile from Braeburn and off Charter Road. It was the essence of a suburban childhood. The street was full of kids. On the right side were two girls, Emma and Amelia. Emma was my age, with light brown hair and freckles that spotted her round face. Amelia was taller, with long blonde hair that swooped down her back. Amelia was my brother's age and on rare occasions the four of us would hang out, but usually it was just Emma and me.

On the left side was a boy a few years younger than me named Liam. He had a short temper and would often run home crying if he didn't get his way. Liam was the kind of kid whose emotions could be read just by the look on his face. He also had a little baby sister named Ava, who melted the hearts of all the parents in the neighborhood. She had curly blonde hair and a face that would scrunch up at the sound of the ice cream truck approaching. She could have easily been on television; she was that cute. We would all meet in the cul-de-sac and play dead or alive, hide and seek, and truth or dare. A few houses down was an elderly Italian couple whose grandkids would play us in baseball whenever they came to town.

My sister Mattie was always following me around, but I didn't mind; I loved her. She is four and a half years younger than me and wanted to go everywhere I went. Mattie had a lot of my mother's characteristics. She worked hard in school and got straight A's all throughout lower, middle, and upper school. She was always bound for success. She had dark brown hair and light hazelnut eyes. She was both a girl's girl and a tomboy. She loved her Vera Bradley bags and wearing makeup, but she also loved to play sports like basketball and football. She didn't mind getting dirty or pushed down during Red Rover; having two older brothers made her tough. I'd outfit her with full body pads to play goalie during street hockey and then proceeded to send her my strongest slap shots.

There was a one-eyed cat that crept around houses and got into fights with my dog, Gus. The cat always won. We got Gus shortly after my first dog, Shiloh, was given away to a farmer on the outskirts of Charlotte. Shiloh was a beagle and was constantly sneaking under the fence and running away. We had gotten him after watching the movie of the same name. Shiloh was meant for a farm, and I believe he lived out his best years there.

Gus was a medium-sized black dog who loved humans but became satanic around other dogs. The dude saw red and bit right at the legs and throat. He was going for the kill. You would have never guessed it by looking at him. He had big brown eyes and a small white spot on his chest that was his sweet spot. My mom brought him home after one of her students rescued a litter. She couldn't resist and adopted him on the spot. At that time, we also had a golden retriever named Sandy. She was a sweet dog but had temperament issues. The important thing was that she and Gus got along. Growing up with dogs showed me the importance they played in a human's life. This sentiment would ring especially true in my mid-twenties. Benji would come into my life and provide one of the few stable surfaces to lean against through years of alcohol and drug abuse. Without saying a word, he kept me safe.

He never left my side, even when I pushed him away. Benji became my guardian angel.

The house on Kenyon Court had a pool, so our Rama Swim Club member tags were no longer needed. We had a club right in the backyard and the neighbors came over regularly to use it. I'd usually find Liam and Ava standing at the gate entrance with puppy dog eyes, just waiting to jump in. Charlotte summer days made the pool the prime breeding ground for activity. We'd have pool parties and cookouts and see who could make the biggest splashes off the diving board.

Nine feet deep, the cleaning octopus crept— its long blue dotted tail wagged back and forth, eating all of Kenyon Court's foliage. I used to put a bucket over my head like a saltwater scuba diver searching for sponges. Both sets of grandparents lived near Tarpon Springs, and I had been there a few times to eat Greek food and go to the beach.

I'd sit up in my top corner room at night and gaze at the dark abyss of the pool. *What lay in there? Would it climb the red brick wall and up into my room?* I usually kept the blinds closed, unless the pool light was on or my dad was having a party. The smell of tiki torches usually sent the signal.

Beyond the pool and behind the fence was a wooded area. In the deep corner was a mud mound covered in grass where I'd pretend to be a WWI fighter. I'd grab pebbles and throw them over, sometimes hitting the cars going by. I'd quickly duck my head under or run away.

Emma and Amelia had a trampoline, where night after night, I wanted to lay. Have you ever sat still on a trampoline? Try it. Double bounces weren't important. I wasn't interested in flips. I just wanted to look up. I'd sit there and think. *Where would I go and what would I do?* It helped that Emma was next to me. Although it was adolescent love, it mattered. Her house was bigger than mine, and it mattered. She had an N64 for crying out loud, and we'd play Golden-Eye for hours.

After my dad made me mow the grass on that awfully slanted hill, I'd always look over to the window above the garage where her playroom was. She wasn't there. I'd ride my roller blades in circles and wait for her to walk down her driveway. I'd sell lemonade at the end of the street in hopes that she'd come help me. I was always too afraid to phone her house. I liked her a lot but never expressed it. I wonder how she's doing now.

Me and my brother's relationship was always on the fringe growing up and the challenge of connecting with him got to me over time. His professional wrestling obsession lent itself to DDTs and sleeper holds performed on his favorite opponent—me. I'd cry out to mom and he'd call me a tattle tale, followed by a dead arm.

We'd rent a console from Blockbuster and choose two games that we'd play until Sunday. It was always a big deal. Drew would hog the controller or straight up obliterate me in the games we rented.

He'd play me in a game of horse or one on one, and always beat me five to nil. Despite all of this, I still loved him. I just wanted to connect with him.

We moved two more times before I left the suburbs. Two more moves that defined eighteen. I left high school with high hopes, with dreams that soon fleeted with the places I went, the people I met, and the decisions I made. They said it would be easy growing up, and I believed them. They said I would be successful after college, but I still wasn't. Picking up the pieces would have to start eventually.

2

Writing in Reverse

My childhood was wonderful, but on that December day in 2018, it was dark. It was a week before Christmas, and I had been sitting and staring out the small window for days. It was the only window in the attic room, dirty and hard to see out of. It was worn, just like me. The glass was thin and air pushed through the cracked frame. It was the only thing that distracted me from the hell I was living in. I lived in that room before. Brief stints between periods of sobriety and the hell of addiction. I took handfuls of Lorazepam and gulped down bottles of whiskey, blacking out for hours at a time, pissing into empty Gatorade bottles, and throwing out loads of empty beer cans onto the grass below. I stayed up all night on the Adderall I stole from my dad's medicine cabinet watching COPS on YouTube and blew marijuana smoke into the closet. I hid liquor bottles in every corner to cover up the lies I told my parents about being sober. I created oil paintings to give to lovers and rolled around in paint-stained clothes, sobbing like a baby once the relationship fell apart. But this time would be different. I told myself enough was enough. No more lying. No more stealing. No more drugs or alcohol. Was a failed engagement not enough to stop me? I was sure this was the last rock bottom.

My body was beaten. Sore. I had aches and sharp pain. My eyes were droopy and my throat hurt. I stared at every crevice of ripped white paint and every dot along the speckled popcorn ceiling. There were small holes scattered throughout the yellowed wall from my previous attempts to hang up art and make it a home. Nothing about the room was inviting. I sat and wondered who had lived there before me. Had it been a child? The ceiling was low, so it would have made sense. Or had it been a simple storage area, a place where the previous owners put the things they never used? My parents rarely went up there. It was an unused space that now became my room, again.

I felt cold inside. Cold from what I did to Emily. But I still had an angry, hot, outer shell that could have boiled over at any minute. She didn't deserve a verbal thrashing, but how could she have done that to me? How could she have called the wedding off? I was pointing the finger at her. It was her fault, not mine. I thought she could have stayed. She could have helped me overcome my addictions. But no, she had given up and left me to fend for myself. She had finally thrown in the towel.

She was still in the house we shared in the valley on Boscobel. She was still driving along the east Nashville streets I so graciously stumbled home drunk on. I wondered what she was doing. What she was thinking. I wondered if she missed me. A mixture of 'I love you' and 'fuck you' swirled through my brain. I wanted to call her. I wanted to text her. But I knew she wouldn't answer. She had picked up the phone too many times before, not knowing where I was and when I was coming home. She had given me everything she could and was tapped out. She didn't want to talk to me and I couldn't blame her. Sorry wasn't going to fix this problem. Apologies from my mouth meant nothing anymore.

I hadn't slept on a twin-sized bed since I was a kid. At six foot five, I just didn't fit. My legs hung off the end, and the tiny blanket exposed my swollen feet. The circulation to the far corners of my body was strained by the booze. Sleeping became an exhausting task. I'd snap awake from the nightmares drenched in cold sweat and count the time by the pace of the clouds floating by. They were terrifying dreams. Memories of inexcusable actions that only I knew about. I had cheated on her twice during our engagement. Two drunken nights, I went home with a stranger blown out on cocaine. Cheating wasn't right and I knew that, but my addictions had thrown all morals out the window. I was looking for something that could love me more than how much I loved drinking. Unfortunately, nothing would meet that need, not even Emily. The half-hearted, motorcycle-meandering persona I displayed to everyone else was staring right back at me and I didn't like what I saw.

I moved back home out of necessity. I had nowhere else to go, and my parents were nice enough to accept me back. I sat there mulling over how I got there. It had been years since I'd thought about everything I'd done. I was in a perpetual cycle of alcohol and drug abuse. My mind was clouded, gray, just like the Nashville sky I was staring at. It was a typical pallet for winter. I was broken by circumstances brought on by no one other than myself. It was a hard realization to admit guilt. But I had really done it this time.

I still hadn't unpacked my bags. I didn't have many things, and they all fit into my car in one go. I had gotten used to being on the run. Living in a place for a few months, avoiding collection calls and 'friends' I screwed over, leaving before anyone knew I was gone; it was a familiar cycle. I packed fast, and was sure I left a few things behind. Whatever it was, it wasn't important. I was too angry to care about material things.

The bare-bone branches of winter didn't make me feel much better. I had no desire to go anywhere. Where would I go? I knew every road in the neighborhood, it was nothing new, and everything reminded me of her. How could I start over? How could I wipe the slate clean?

The previous night, I laid in bed, the soft white of the moon casting a diagonal contrast across my chest. I was hoping for stars but couldn't see any. I kept looking out and wondering how I ended up there at twenty-eight. That wasn't the plan.

The streets were quiet. No one walked by for hours. Normally there would be people running, walking their dog, or pushing their kids in strollers doing the normal necessities of life. But I was stuck just like the elderly neighbor next door. She'd leave the lamp on in her upstairs room, but I never saw her. I wondered if she was happy. I wondered what she was doing there. Maybe knitting or watching television. Maybe cooking or calling her loved ones. Her dog was certainly loud. That fucking thing never stopped barking. It was always outside, running in circles and creating a ruckus. Maybe I did the same thing. It didn't seem to work for him either.

I didn't want to normalize the situation. I was an adult, for crying out loud. I should have been out making moves, going places, but I couldn't. I was broke. Not a dime or a dollar in my pocket. I had quit my art teaching job three weeks before, a bit of information that I hid from Emily. I'd wake up in the morning and leave for 'work,' only to make a big loop around town while she actually went to her job. I'd stop by the liquor store and start drinking by 8:30 a.m. I had the entire day to waste, and I did it by watching endless videos on the internet. To this day, I can't remember what I watched.

She eventually found out when she came home from lunch and saw me plastered on the bed in the back room, slouched over my computer. Needless to say, she'd find out about all my stunts. Just a month earlier she took the trash out and noticed a pile of liquor bottles and beer cans shoved at the bottom of the bag. I'd normally take the trash out to avoid detection, but forgot that particular morning. My sobriety facade soon faded, and she retreated in doubt.

I was showing up to work for months hungover and high. I tried to teach kids the foundations of making art but gave up before the ring of the first bell. I was there to make a paycheck. I needed money to keep up with the drinking habits and bar tabs. I needed money to buy the bags of weed and grams of coke. I needed money to take Emily out to dinner in order to mask what was really going on behind her back. I scraped through by doing the bare minimum, sitting at the front of the room with my head down while kids counted how many likes they had on their Instagram page. The assistant principal was on to me. He knew I didn't care, but as long as I showed up to work, there wasn't much he could do besides crush me on my observations. Luckily, the art class was normally the last thing on the administration's mind. It made it easy to fly under the radar.

"David, dinner is ready!" I heard my mom call.

Calling me like a seven year old school boy whose meat and three was warm and waiting. It was about six o'clock by then, dinner time for many. I had barely eaten all day, but I wasn't hungry. What had I fed lately besides my ego? I didn't feel like feeding that anymore.

I just couldn't see how I could change. I had done the same thing every day for years—drinking and smoking weed every chance I got. It didn't matter if I was about to go to work, church, or a funeral, I was getting fucked up. Nothing was done sober. I had essentially spent my entire adulthood so far in a chemically-induced haze. You had pills, I ate them. You had acid, I tripped. You bought shots, I was taking them. There was no limit to what I would say yes to. Emily was just an accessory to the madness.

My body spent almost every day with her, but my mind was far away. I assumed she'd go along with it forever. But behavior like that has time stamps. I promised to change, but failed miserably in a matter of days, even hours. They were such empty spews of good faith. Maybe I scared her when I was hunched over the toilet those many nights. But no matter what, I couldn't stop. I didn't want to.

My t-shirt reeked of regret, and the colorful paint stains across it seemed like a metaphor for my behavior. I smeared it without a care. All my clothes were like that, well, whatever clothes I had left. I trashed so many things, most of them given to me by people who loved me. Yet what did I give them in return? The answer was absolutely nothing.

"David, it's getting cold!" My mom yelled again.

She hated when I was slow to the table. She hated that I was upstairs all by myself. But being in the attic room had become a cyclic part of my life. It wasn't the first time I was up there, and it wouldn't be the last. It was the only place anyone knew where to put me when shit hit the fan. It was the only place where I could retreat from all the destruction I caused. I had to go downstairs. I had to show my face.

What had I done?

3

Born in Love

I was born to two people that were madly in love with one another, a mom and dad who wanted to make a family in North Carolina. They welcomed me into the world with joy. My mother had been a teacher for many years before I was born. She was a natural educator, who followed in her own mom's footsteps to the front of the class. She was good at her job, and year after year, her students would revisit her classroom. But being a mother was more important than any class she taught.

Growing up, she would do anything for me, but my addiction became something even she struggled to grapple with. It didn't make sense. How could a kid who grew up in a loving home shatter their life with drugs and alcohol? How could an educated person fall into the hands of addiction? My addiction had torn her apart slowly and left her helpless. But there's something about a mother's love that remains unshakable through it all. Through sleepless nights, mountains of anxiety, heartache, and sharp anger, she always managed to hang onto hope. She prayed endlessly that God would keep me safe and break me from addiction. Even when I denied his existence, she'd send me early morning texts of scripture in hopes I'd start my day on a positive note. I wouldn't realize until years later how much those 5 a.m. pings on my cell phone would mean.

I grew up in my mother's fifth grade classroom. I'd take the bus from the lower school campus to the separate middle school campus, sitting behind a bus driver named Mel. His name always reminded me of the koala Beanie Baby. The other faculty kids and I would play with our Tamagotchis and clean up the shit from our screens. We'd trade Pokemon cards and sing the song about the place in France where the naked ladies dance. There were little worries about the world passing by, and I knew in a few minutes, I'd see my mom in her familiar classroom.

It was a short ten-minute ride, and I always got off excited to see her. We stayed late most days, so she could finish up her work. During that time, I'd draw on her overhead projector using colorful Visa V markers. Her classroom was a creator's paradise. She had stacks of construction paper, buckets of colored pencils, large white poster boards, plain scissors, patterned scissors, glue, tape, magazines, books, mechanical pencils, Gelly Rolls, glitter, stickers and cardboard. Her room fostered my creative side from day one. She was proud to have a kid interested in the arts, and along with her dad (Papa), supported my artistic ability through private art lessons.

I'd run around campus with the other faculty kids. We'd sneak into the teachers' lounge and look in the fridge; we'd shoot basketball in the gym and watch the seventh and eighth grade teams practice; and we'd explore the muddy creek where we raced our rubber band propeller boats during science lab. When I was tired, I'd return to my mom's classroom and get a soda from the mini fridge and a piece of candy from the reward jar in the closet. By that point, it was usually time to go home.

My mother cared greatly about my education and always made sure grammar was a top priority—she was an English teacher after all. She also taught American history and had endless books on America's wars and its struggles. I learned a lot just by looking at the pictures, and it grew my fascination with the past. It's funny how history seemed to repeat itself. The horror of the human condition played itself out on the images in front of me. It was dark, it was real, and it captured my attention. Humans could be the most loving creatures, yet also the most terrifying. As a kid, it was hard to reconcile that people could have both sides, but I'd later find out the mind and body are very pliable things. It didn't take much to go from one to the other, especially under the intoxication of drugs and alcohol.

My papers were always properly edited, even in elementary school, and she helped me develop my Science Fair idea of figuring out which color M&M averaged the most pieces in a series of packs. She'd stay up late into the night and help me with my math problems and wouldn't give up until I solved the problems correctly on my own. She was a mother who taught me the value of education, even when I couldn't see it myself. All the teachers knew her and had her number on speed dial. That kept me straight and out of trouble.

I attended Charlotte Country Day School, a private school with top-notch teachers and facilities. We had a library stocked with books, a gym with endless gear, an auditorium with a glossy wooden stage, and playground equipment that seemed to stretch for miles. Free tuition was a perk of being a teacher's child. I would have never been able to attend otherwise. Grades were small, around one hundred and thirty students, and most were "lifers," a term used to describe students who attended from kindergarten through twelfth grade. It wasn't a very racially diverse school; there were only a handful of black and Asian kids in my grade level. It was a white-washed experience with extremely privileged kids.

The only real dive into other ethnicities came through basketball. I made the Charlotte Nets, an AAU basketball team that practiced on the north side of town. I was the only white kid on the team, and the experience was a sharp contrast from school life. We had basketball in common, but the material difference between the kids I went to school with and the kids I played basketball with was stark. It was the underlying difference that was never really talked about amongst my peers and me. But that was the innocent beauty of being a kid. It wouldn't be clear until later in life how privileged I was.

The cost of tuition at Country Day was about fifteen thousand dollars per year, making it the most expensive private school in Charlotte. It had two campuses that sprawled over acres of land and resembled a college campus. It was a school for the kids of doctors, lawyers, and CEOs.

I remember going over to friends' houses to hang out. Their houses were huge; we're talking mansions. The kind of houses with columns in the front and six bedrooms and five baths. My friends wore the newest clothes and shoes. I remember feeling jealous of the ones that had the Nikes with the air bubbles and the Abercrombie and Fitch pants that zipped off into shorts. I'd go over to my friend Ethan's house and ask to change into his clothes. Ethan was a down-to-earth kid whose life revolved around tennis. He was good, I mean really good, and spent a lot of his free time training at the local racquet club. Ethan's father had passed away, and it was easy to tell he and his mom had a special bond. The loss of his dad was something he never really talked about. I always wondered but didn't know how to approach it. I had never experienced such trauma in my life.

Ethan and I connected like most little boys do. We played Crash Bandicoot on his Playstation, launched tennis balls over the roof of his house, and stuffed our clothes until we looked like sumo wrestlers. It all felt normal until we loaded into his mom's Jaguar and drove to Charlotte Country Club. It was that clear line between them and me that became more and more evident as I rose through the grades. It wasn't like my family was poor, but these friends were next-level rich.

My mom always made my birthdays special and made sure I had plenty of friends at every party. There were pirate parties where we bobbed for apples and played baseball in the cul-de-sac. Parties at Chuck-E-Cheese's and Celebration Station. I always had candles and a cake. She made sure I got a few dollars under my pillow when I lost a tooth and a basket full of chocolate when the Easter bunny came. She made sure gifts were under the Christmas tree and that my special elf, Sparkle, left me treats around the house. She kept the magic of childhood alive and kept me safe from the realities of the world.

Long hugs at night and bedtime stories, usually from my children's Bible, were a nightly occurrence. She made sure I knew that God loved me, even though I had no grasp of what that meant. I could never understand that as a kid. How could an invisible being love me more than the flesh and bones that made me?

Family dinners were important to her and I plainly remember her calling, "Food is hot!" If I wasn't there in thirty seconds, I was in trouble; after all, she did put the time in to make it. We would all sit around the table and talk about upcoming rec basketball and soccer games or homework and projects that were due soon. My dad would usually break the silence with a loud fart. He's funny like that. When we finished, my siblings and I were responsible for cleaning up and loading the plates in the dishwasher. It was one of the many things we were responsible for in order to get a small allowance. It was her way of teaching us some sense of responsibility.

I never really saw my mom and dad fight with each other, but if they did, it was sometimes because my dad got too drunk. They made sure to always do it behind closed doors. It never lasted long, and they both would apologize soon after it ended. They never held grudges and were forgiving of one another. As I grew older, I knew that disagreements were inevitable but learned that forgiveness was key to a clear conscience and a healthy relationship. I learned that grudges were the foundation of endless anger. But I'd later find that healing comes in different forms and at different times. Healing couldn't be rushed.

My mother made sure we saw all the enjoyments of life. It was important to her that I wasn't left behind. She took me to museums, the zoo, the park, and the movies. She took me to the mountains and the beach and Washington, D.C. She made sure I knew the beauty of the natural world and that everything around me was from a power greater than myself. I came to enjoy the outdoors and spent a lot of my time running around our suburban neighborhood. It's a love of the outdoors that I still have today.

She was a soft-hearted mother who knew how to hold me when I was sad, but stern enough to teach me right from wrong. When I did something wrong or talked back, she was sure to correct it fast. She built my moral compass from the ground up. She took me to Florida to see Nanny and Papa. Her mom was almost an exact reflection of her. Deeply religious, kind, calm, and loving.

Nanny and Papa were very active in our lives and would drive up from Florida in their Vanagon at least twice a year. We'd sleep in the camper and wait for Santa Claus to come and watch television in the back seat on long hauls. They loved their grandchildren and Nanny wore a necklace with her grandkids' birthstones sprinkled across it; mine was aquamarine.

It was important to my mom that I knew them. She wanted me to know where her character was born. It became clear to me that Nanny shaped my mother into the person she had become. My mother tried to do the same with me, but my life and my decisions had other plans.

My mom was present at everything. From sports games to field trips, she made sure I knew she cared. She drove me to sleepovers, theater productions, and holiday celebrations all across Charlotte. I know it was hard on her. She was busy and had a life of her own, but she never showed it. Her uncanny ability to handle stress always impressed me, but it was her faith that drove her through the stopped traffic.

My mom is a researcher. She reads about everything and searches for answers through words. During the years of addiction and chaos, she retreated into the books she read. She'd buy me books with eerily similar stories to mine, but I never once opened them. I thought I could handle circumstances on my own. I didn't need to read about how other people overcame their demons. To me, I had it all down. I knew it all. Despite my fierce denial, she'd continue to tell me about what she read.

I can still find her early in the morning at the front of the house finding answers in the books she reads. Her quiet time is her meditation time and before the sun rises above the horizon, she's given grace to a day that has yet to happen. I've learned to wake up early and respect the dusk of thought as well. It took me many years to understand the importance of reading positive messages. I knew during all those mornings I was waiting outside the liquor store to open, she was praying over me. She found peace in that, and I pushed her away.

She guided me through college applications and helped me navigate the countless college campus tours. She did mock interviews and helped me develop the appropriate questions to ask during an interview. She did everything she could to set me up for success in life.

But as I entered college, the strong relationship we had growing up soon cracked as my life took a spiral downward. I pushed her away and demanded I trudge my own path. I was too proud, but deep down, I was lost. She never came to visit because I didn't invite her. I thought I had my shit together, but my facade melted away and crumbled under piles of shame and regret. I didn't feel worthy of the love she showed me my entire life.

I left holiday visits early out of spite and ignored phone calls and text messages. I felt like I didn't deserve anything except the failures I accepted. I knew I was crushing her slowly, but she still loved me. She still called me. She still helped me if I was hungry. To her, I was still her son. To me, I was a son that wrote too many wrongs. But despite everything, my mother's love could never fade. It would be one of the few things that remained unconditional.

4

Wrenched Terror

It was only the second night home after shit hit the fan. I woke up, freezing, from a terrible night's sleep. I was sweating in places I didn't know I could. My body couldn't decide if it was hot or cold. It was a night full of terrors. I dreamed about people and places I hadn't thought of in ages. People I'd hurt and people I'd dodged. It had gotten easy to fabricate stories. Big or small, it didn't matter. It was second nature.

I tossed and turned and must have woken up at least fifteen times to change shirts. The drunken monster was relentless and wouldn't let go of my body. It was fighting for space and asking for another drink. It was thirsty and my brain was telling me to give in. I told myself to hold out for one more minute. It was an endless battle of yes and no. I wasn't sure how long I could last.

The Nashville sky tossed and turned with high winds and purple golden clouds that couldn't seem to sit still. I didn't drink the night before. It was the first time in years my body had fallen asleep without its special sauce. It begged for one last drop to fall in the bottomless pit, and the tips of my fingers shook for one last go. It had become the gas that ran my motor and it numbed me to sleep so well. I hadn't dreamed with such clarity in ages. There was no more booze to blur the line between the reality I was avoiding and the lie I was living.

Was all the pain my mind and body were going through worth getting sober? My mind was telling me no. It played tricks on me every minute of the day. It told me I was weak and to just give in. It told me I was boring and unlovable. It told me to love no one else. It was convincing, almost too good at its job. But I knew that feeling would be short-lived and eventually drop me back off where I started. I knew how the story ended in the past, but if I had just one drink, what difference would it make? I could stop, right?

I laid in bed for hours. I had no plans that day, no people to see, no job to go to. No one to call and no one to answer to. Although the bed was uncomfortable, it was the only thing that could hold my sluggish body. My back and legs ached, and my toes curled like a worm on the end of a fishing hook. My parents and I were under the same roof, but in different headspaces. I couldn't muster the energy to talk to my family. There'd be no topic that could cheer me up.

My brother had arrived earlier than expected after the news broke. Emily had already left Nashville, and it was just me in the Boscobel apartment. I was spending the last few days there, sitting in the memories. I tore through it like a hurricane. There was trash everywhere, empty liquor bottles and piles of pot on every corner of the counter. I was contemplating on whether or not to snort the rest of the coke in one giant line and call it goodbye, but something stopped me. I was miserable but I wasn't ready to overdose, at least, not on purpose.

Drew got there that evening with shock and confusion on his face. Just a few weeks earlier, Emily and I seemed fine. We stood there in silence hugging each other. Two brothers that up until that point had barely talked to each other, let alone touched each other. It was a moment where I knew my big brother loved me, flaws and all. It was a moment where he knew I had a major addiction problem. He had shown up. He was there. It was like two brothers acknowledging each other for the first time.

My heart rate pounded with inconsistency when I thought about Emily. She had gone back to North Carolina for the holidays. She went back to be with her family who knew nothing of my addiction. Emily had kept it from them. Maybe she was embarrassed. Maybe she thought it would get better.

I tricked her family into playing my game. I'd sit at their kitchen table and tell them I would take care of her and give her everything I could. Keeping her safe would be my priority. Yet, I put myself and the bottle in the forefront.

I went to pre-wedding parties hosted by people from her childhood church. I stayed at her aunt and uncle's house in Raleigh where I stole pain pills from the medicine cabinet. I went to her family's vacation home at the beach where I threw wine bottles off the dock in a drunken fit. I traveled to Fort Worth, Texas, where we stayed with her brother and met his adopted kid from China.

Her brother would find out for himself just how bad my situation was. I was miserable for the three days we stayed there. I kept my composure for as long as I could. But I could only hold my addiction in for so long. All hell broke loose on the last night. Her brother offered me some of his finer whiskey, and I took it without hesitation. It was already forty-eight hours of sober hell. I drank one, then two, then three. How many I took after that, I don't know. The night was a blur and I woke up the next day wearing all my clothes and laying sideways on the guest room bed. Emily was already awake and sitting on the living room couch, her face full of disappointment. I had no idea what I said or did.

Understandably, Emily was pissed, and we took a walk around the neighborhood where she would give me an ultimatum. I had to put the bottle down or things were over. But like most alcoholics do, I talked my way out of the situation, manipulating her into thinking I would get help. You see, alcoholics are smooth talkers and she gave me one last pass. I, of course, had no plans of getting help, but knew it would cool the conversation down temporarily.

We got on the plane back to Nashville with a subtle understanding that things wouldn't work out. She wanted to believe in me, but I didn't believe in myself. The relationship, the engagement, would be over in a matter of days. I had been acting out for months, ignoring her heart-wrenching pleas for me to get help.

She would leave that Tuesday, just two days after returning from Texas. Held up in the house on a bender, I practically drank myself into oblivion. Random faces that flashed on and off of bar stools. I must've blown through a thousand dollars, the remaining amount of my last teaching paycheck. I couldn't remember who I talked to, where I went, or how I got home. I couldn't remember taking care of Benji, if he was fed or if he had water. *Did I drive*

my car? Did I text and call Emily and leave vengeful messages?
Did I call my parents or send angry emails to my old boss?

My sketchbook was full of empty line drawings and
scribbles that ran off the side of the page. It was full of Sharpie
marks that bled through the back and colors that didn't match. I
lost my creative way and needed to live in reality.

I thought I was cool, riding around on my motorcycle and
acting like I had no one to answer to. I was the star of the show and
everyone else was there to serve me. My language was twisted and
slurred. I could probably guess where I went—Lipstick Lounge,
Vinyl Tap, or somewhere in between on Gallatin Road. I'd
recognize other patrons at the bar, hugging them like I hadn't seen
them in years and asking them how their day was. I'd get half-
hearted answers that skirted the truth and were topped off with a
round of shots.

I had seen the same people out for years, but didn't know a
thing about them beyond their favorite drink and the prices of the
drugs they sold. Any aspect of their lives outside of the bar was a
mystery. Mine was no different. We were all running from the
biggest problems in our lives, and that problem was ourselves.

I attached to people based on what they could give me. I
was just another fool willing to give their entire paycheck for a fast
track to an early grave. Both sides were playing one another, but in
my addict mind, I was winning.

I destroyed all of the art I created over the past ten years. I
put knives through canvases and tore sketchbook pages in half.
Drawings were thrown in the trash, and the catalog was deleted off
my computer. I was a creator crossed in a slanted state of mind. It
was art created in a time I tried to forget, yet, the memories hadn't
left me.

The few spared pieces were in my friend Riley's hands by
that point. She always appreciated the things I'd create. Her
apartment was full of my art. Maybe one day, I'd see it again. I
knew she was taking care of it.

There was a bruise on my leg from God knows what,
probably from running into a bar stool or bathroom stall. I smelled

like the bottom of an ashtray, and the bottom of my eyes were black. When you're up all night, you lose track of today because there is nothing to do but think about yesterday. It was a sick pattern that turned your brain into a raisin. I still had a few numbers in my phone, mostly powder and green sources. But now that my money was gone, I'm sure they wouldn't answer.

I was down and out. I was knocked around and sore. *Did they care about my emotionally distraught and soulless state? Did they care that my wedding got called off and my girl left me? Did they care that I couldn't sleep?* I think not. I was no better than the man sitting on the stool next to me.

My 'friends' barely knew Emily because I never talked about her. She got to the point where she wouldn't go out in the madness. She didn't like the people I was with. She had a natural intuition, but my overbearing drunken self always downplayed her concern. I was hanging around people who cared little for the woman I had proposed to. But they were my connection to coke, Adderall, molly, and a good time.

I defended my 'friends' when she said she got bad vibes from them. She had a point, but I didn't care. I was doing what I wanted. I was having my cake and eating it too. I brought them over to our house where we snorted lines as she slept in the back room. My only goal was to get as fucked up as possible. The girl I said, "I love you" to meant nothing to me by that point.

So, I just laid in bed in the attic room. It was early and I was still on teacher time. But I had no class to teach, no students to help. My mom was probably sitting in her chair in the front of the house wondering what I was doing, what I was thinking, and what my next steps were going to be. They were going to want to know. I still hadn't canceled my honeymoon reservation; I was delaying the inevitable.

It was almost Christmas. There were wreaths on the windows and presents under the tree. Christmas had been a time of celebration. A time when I was too excited to sleep. Christmas was always a special time but as my drinking progressed through my mid-twenties, I'd wake up on Christmas morning hungover and feeling like shit.

It started out innocently. Your typical family get-together where drinks are poured and old stories from childhood get passed around. It was supposed to be fun but for me, getting shit-faced was a requirement. How else would I connect with my family? It was a skewed take on old holiday traditions.

I needed to change clothes. They were still stuffed in the trash bags I threw them in. The attic room only had a few pieces of furniture, most of it my grandad's. He would buy us strange gifts off late night infomercials, like used Polish army underwear and fart machines, oversized sweatshirts and odd figurines. I could have used some of his strange humor at that moment. Maybe 'pulling his finger' one last time would cut the stale air.

I could smell dinner creeping its way up the stairs. There was never a shortage of food to eat, especially during the holidays. The smell was making my stomach growl. All I normally ate was television dinners and shitty bar food. It was a healthy diet of salty foods and cocaine and both were seeping their way from my pores.

But my stomach wasn't growling because I was hungry. It was turning for a substance ever since I got home. What started as a novelty became a necessity and not giving into temptation was getting harder.

I had a future that looked bright at eighteen. A future with endless possibilities. But I no longer viewed my life that way. My life had been narrowed down to one thing—drugs—and they had dumped me in a delta of depression. I was fucked up in the head and reflecting on how stupid I'd been. I wanted to write a letter to Emily and to other people I hurt. But I wasn't sure what to say. It was too early for forgiveness and too late to say sorry.

"David, why don't you come downstairs?" my mom yelled.

I needed to get my shit together. I needed to go downstairs. I needed to show them that I appreciated them. I certainly hadn't done that in years.

5

The Blade

It took me thirty-one years to see how alike me and my dad are.

He grew up in Roanoke, Virginia, with his mom, dad, and older brother. My dad was a tough kid who got into a lot of trouble, but he had sports to keep him in line. Basketball was his game. He was number one on his high school team and earned a scholarship to play at Randolph-Macon College. Ironically, he failed physical education, mainly for skipping class.

He'd coach my recreation teams growing up and was tough on us during practice, making us run suicides when we would miss an easy jumper or didn't use our weakside hand on a layup. Basketball was our place for connection. Every house we moved to had a basketball net, and I would stay up late into the evening shooting hoops. He taught me proper form and ball-handling skills. He signed me up for basketball camps and took me to tryouts. Every Saturday morning meant a basketball game and post-game meal at Phil's Deli in Strawberry Hill. My dad loved breakfast, and it soon became my favorite meal of the day too. He instilled in me a determination to get better at the sport and to have pride in success.

Growing up, he'd drive me to school every Friday morning, and we'd stop at the Exxon gas station on Providence Road to get a donut and a biscuit. On the way there, we'd listen to classic rock bands like The Marshall Tucker Band, Lynyrd Skynyrd, and Creedence Clearwater Revival. Other days, we'd listen to "The Big Show" with John Boy and Billy and I always tried to imagine what their faces looked like. Those Fridays were special, not because we got pastries, but because I got to spend time with him. He always called me D-Man, and to this day, he still does. It's his way of letting me know he loves me.

My dad worked in the biggest building in Charlotte, the Bank of America building. Its spires shot into the heavens and looked down upon the colorful canopy of Charlotte. As a kid, I admired the building as it glistened above the clouds. He would eventually take me to his office. I walked in the lobby and stared at the marble columns and giant front desk where the security officers sat. There were at least fifteen elevators. The amount of floors baffled me, and I thought everyone that worked there was important. I wanted to go to the top floor, stationed like a gargoyle, and try to find my house amongst the millions. My dad was larger than life and the fact that he worked in the tallest building made him feel untouchable. It must have been inspiring to work in such a place. It had such grandeur.

He eventually started his own business. It was something he always wanted to do. I'd visit him in his office where he was constantly on the phone with clients. The walls in his office were lined with the artwork I'd create. He was proud to have a son with a creative side.

He'd teach me how to drive. With him in the passenger seat, I'd drive around the neighborhood as he coached me the best way he knew how. He always taught me to "anticipate," a word that became a part of the 'Andy-ism' list. He'd eventually give me a list of twenty-one "Lessons from Andy" at Christmas. These included things like finding a local repair shop, taking one Prilosec every morning, volunteering, tithe to a church, making a will, and many others. They were his life lessons, so to speak.

Although my dad was a tough businessman and became quite successful at what he did, he has an extremely soft side to him. He's a dad who shows his emotions, and at many holiday dinners, when we picked a family member out of a hat and wrote a letter to them, he'd cry over the one written to him. We all did. My parents were never afraid to show their heartfelt emotion in front of me. He showed me it was okay to be soft when appropriate.

Now you're probably wondering why this chapter is called 'The Blade,' so, let me tell you. I want you to imagine the most knee-jerk reacting Canadian, one who wears socks with sandals, and loves cheese curds. A guy who flips out. A spaz. The kind of guy you can't give one ounce of advice to. Well, this guy would be my granddad, my dad's father. He was a gospel singer who cussed at nothing and flipped out on you for no apparent reason. He was a guy who was a total hard ass and difficult to get along with. This type of person has a name in the Newson family, and it's a gene most of us don't want. It's a slight deformation in the genetic series called the blade. I luckily avoided the gene, but my dad got a hefty amount. It's mostly a term used in a 'bless your heart' type of way. My dad is the second blade in a long lineage, and from my observations, he passed a little to my older brother too. We all still crack jokes about granddad, the OG blade, to this day.

As I grew older, I stepped away from sports and developed a bigger interest in film, painting, and other creative arts. Although my dad didn't really understand what I was creating, he backed me wholeheartedly. He's the kind of dad that supported whatever endeavor I wanted to pursue, showing up at my gallery shows and film festivals and helping me purchase the necessary equipment to chase it properly.

My dad was constantly lifting me up and bringing me out of bouts of depression. Making game plans and constantly talking me through the barriers I hit. He'd come up with new career ideas and give me numbers to people that might help in the process of finding employment. He knew what it was like to work hard for what you wanted and knew it wouldn't come easy.

I didn't learn about his substance use until I was an adult. He had used cocaine during the eighties and nineties, but it got to the point where he realized he was not going down the right path and it would lead to the destruction of himself and his family. I'm not totally sure when or why he started, but I assume it was during his college years. And like me, it continued well after his schooling days. However, when presented with this fork, he stopped using drugs completely and committed to his marriage and children.

Drinking was an activity he'd participate in quite regularly when I was a kid. He'd have parties in the backyard and go out to bars to watch sports games. I would sometimes go out with him and absorb the drinks in front of me with my young eyes. Alcohol was always around and in the fridge.

Once I turned twenty, the drinking train left the station. It started light but eventually got heavier, graduating from beer to liquor. I'd go out and drink with him. I liked exploring new places, and he enjoyed showing me different dive bars around town.

When I dropped sports, I felt like my dad and I didn't have much in common, but drinking became something we both liked to do. It made me feel closer to him and the alcohol opened me up more. We'd have a good laugh about childhood days, and it sometimes led to smoking a bowl of bud. We'd talk into the night and would crack jokes about extended family. We'd often wake up with a hangover, more so me, and I wouldn't remember most of the conversation. Looking back, the talks were fairly empty. What was the point in bonding when I didn't remember it?

In my mid-twenties, I was far from him. It naturally occurred through the downing of high gravity beers and vodka tonics. My dad knew something was going on, but there was nothing he could do. There was nothing anyone could do. Our lives became two distant relatives. Although he was downstairs, he still felt far away. And although he tried to reach out to me, I kept pushing him away.

In some ways, I blamed him for where I was. Why hadn't he told me about his substance use issues earlier? Why did he go out with me so many times and buy me drinks? Why did he bring out the liquor bottles during Thanksgiving and Christmas? I sat there upset, not just with him, but with everyone else as well. It was everyone else's fault but mine.

But I was looking at my dad from all the wrong angles. Even after rummaging through his drawers, opening his safe, drinking his liquor and lying to him constantly, he still forgave me. And the most fucked up part about it was I'd take before and after pictures on my phone, so I knew exactly how to put back the things I took. I had the act of theft down perfectly, and he was just the right candidate to justify my actions.

But my dad changed. He was able to stop the drug use and minimize his drinking. He put in the work to win my mother. He showed her through his actions, not just the words that came out of his mouth. It set an example for the empty and lost words I was spewing for years. He rose through his own self-destruction. Hearing this once hidden part of my dad's past inspired me to be better, although mine remained empty promises.

I would continue in the same behaviors I promised Emily I'd stop. She was damaged, just like my mom, yet I didn't step up to the plate. I was a person too stuck and stubborn in their own ways. My dad showed me that change was possible, but I hadn't followed his example. I gave up on proving that I could.

I lost that kid who grew up wanting his dad's strength. I lost that kid who wanted his dad's perseverance. I was looking back on the last few years with great regret. I already wasted so much time. So much time chasing highs and short-term thrills that would end with the coming sunrise. I was flawed to the core. My character and my integrity were gone.

6

Back and Forth on Providence Road

We moved to Alexander Hall Drive when I was a freshman in high school. It was a house we lived in for a short while. It was three stories and quite large. We moved a little further out so my brother, Drew, was zoned for Providence High School to play basketball. It was his best shot at being a part of a team that could win and be noticed by college scouts. Charlotte Country Day just didn't have the five-man fighting power. Drew had dreams of playing college ball, but he would party his way opposite that direction. He would become the first child to rebel against the assumed standards. He was at the age where most kids try and find their own way. When the thought of girls and parties took over classroom studies. He always tested the limits but was now fulfilling my parents' worst nightmares. Basketball, which was always my dad's source of pride, was no longer an attainable goal for Drew.

I watched as my brother figured out life on his terms. I watched as his behaviors became real-life problems. He was the first born and the first to make real mistakes. He took the heat for his actions while I sat idle in the background. At that age, getting on someone's bad side wasn't an option for me. I was out to please everyone. To clean up after myself. To do what I was told. To follow the path that was previously set. But Drew showed me indirectly that life could mean many things. That you could take life by the horns and steer it the way you wanted to go. It wouldn't be long before I was doing the same.

Making a life on my own terms. It would become all about me. What I wanted. What I could get. It became a self-fulfilling ego trip that wouldn't stop until everyone around me saw enough. I would go from a people-pleaser to a self-pleaser. What Drew failed to mention was that doing so would mean hurting every person that loved me. Making my own path would have far-reaching consequences.

Drew's mistakes soon became my parent's problems. The house had a basement that became a breeding ground for, let's say, 'youthful growth.' It was easy to get away with things down there. He and his friends would get drunk and piss in the neighbor's bushes and throw beer cans in their yard. They'd litter the place with Taco Bell wrappers after getting the munchies and sneak in girls through the downstairs windows that were previously cracked so the beep of the alarm wouldn't sound late at night.

Drew was a high school kid who was having mostly harmless fun. He was growing up the way a lot of kids do. He would go to college and eventually straighten up his act. He had his faze that faded with the appropriate age. Unfortunately for me, the stop button wouldn't exist, the hallmark of an addict.

While Drew was out with my mom's car, I stayed in my room editing videos on my computer. Videomaking was a new interest for me, sparked by my friend Lucas, who discovered Windows Movie Maker. I had grown up with Lucas since Kindergarten. His dad was the math teacher across the hall from my mom's room and we'd often waste time together drawing on his dad's chalk board as both our parents finished up their work. Lucas had a widow's peak, wore whitewash jeans that didn't quite reach his ankles, and often had whatever t-shirt he was wearing tucked in. He was a smart kid, great at math, but also was on the wrestling team. Lucas and I would hang out until twelfth grade, when the movie making we had started together became the thing that tore us apart. It became a me versus him thing, and I was determined to win the film festival. But getting that title would be the last straw, and I would never hear from Lucas again after graduation.

My friends and I always loved movies, and in fact, spent a whole weekend watching all six Star Wars movies in sequential order. We'd build potato guns out of PVC piping and a grill lighter for a trigger. We'd shoot tennis balls, grapes and hot dogs into the sky for no fucking reason. It was fun, entertaining, and tactile.

Creating things always interested me growing up. It was something away from sports. Something that was different from my brother and dad. Something that could become mine. Art became an outlet that would become a catalyst for my curiosity.

Preferring to draw, edit movies, and build rocket contraptions, you could call me nerdy, but I didn't fit into any sort of group. I swayed from the mathematicians to the science lovers to the sports enthusiasts. I was a walking mixing bowl who hung out with all sorts of different stereotypical high school groups. It didn't matter to me. Sports were always something I did for fun. Something that was normalized. But as the games got more serious and the coaches got more stern, the idea of playing sports was no longer appealing.

After sophomore year, I quit the basketball team after the new coach thought he was taking us to the final four. It was like some sort of road to redemption for him. At 5:30 a.m., he had us in the gym running suicides. By the time class started at 8:15 a.m., I was dead. I'd have to repeat this again after school. He looked like Coach Carter, walking around with his manicured suit and hands. He was a coach trying to whip a bunch of entitled white boys into something they could never be. Our half-time talks were hilarious. He'd pop open the swinging door like a belligerent cowboy and give us a lecture on everything we did wrong. That was followed by silly chalked-up plays he Googled the night before. He was serious and I wasn't.

I held out on football for another year. I was on the scout team, and the coaches acted like your role was important. They really just needed you to be a dummy. I always feared the start of two-a-days in early August and will never forget the raging headaches I'd get every evening. My head wasn't accustomed to such torture, and I took handfuls of Tylenol to get rid of the pain. The upperclassmen would constantly crush me, and the scout team became a dumping ground for their rage. This continued the entire season. But I was too scared to drop it. Coach Turley was intimidating. He'd walk around school with his veiny legs and lazy eye and stare at you while you ate lunch in the cafeteria. He said a lot by saying nothing.

In the weight room, I'd do bench presses, squats, dips and pushups to appease the coaches, and while everyone was eating creatine shakes like candy, I stuck to water. From what I understood, all it did was fill your muscles with water, and I didn't want to pop. It's interesting to think about how scared I was to take supplements back then, especially considering how carefree I'd be with my body just a few years later. It was a youthful fear that would eventually unfold dramatically. I was used to doing things just because I was told to. I fucking hated working out, but I still did it.

We moved again in 2007 when I was a junior in high school. It was the last place in the suburbs of Charlotte I'd live. It was down Providence Road, a half mile from the Arboretum. My parents had moved into the house Nanny and Pappa bought. It was a small house that was barely used since they lived in Florida for most of the year. We moved right before the housing bubble burst in 2008 that bankrupted so many families, and I believe we transferred there to cut back on debt.

The garage became my bedroom. It was a Nickelodeon concept, but I embraced it. I didn't have much of a choice. I had a projector where I'd edit videos and a couch where I got my first hand-job. It was a room that I'd return to a semester into college.

I drove a 1970 Chevrolet Custom truck that was painted red. In the midst of Land Rovers, BMWs, and Mercedes, it was different. It had personality. It was loud as hell and had a V8 engine. I called it Big Red and I'd pick up my prom date in it, wearing a mismatched suit I found at the Sleepy Poet, an antique shop off South Blvd. My AP environmental science teacher would poke fun at it when talking about global warming. The fucking thing definitely wasn't economical but everyone knew Big Red. It made me feel unique at an age when everyone searches for individuality.

Providence Road was the vein that connected all my activities in South Charlotte and I'd drive up and down it late into the night. My friend Henry would throw parties at his house and because I didn't drink at the time, I saw no real reason to be there. I'd leave early with my girlfriend Sophia, and we'd drive around and listen to Coldplay. Like most kids at the time, "A Rush of Blood to the Head" became the soundtrack to our lives. Sophia was an artsy type whom I'd gone to school with since kindergarten. She was a school socialite and rather smart. She was someone I never saw myself dating, but during our AP Studio Art class, we started to click. It was a first love that I never saw coming. And like most young love, it was innocent, playful, and deeply emotional. I had never experienced caring for a girl that way and the feeling sent butterflies in my stomach that couldn't be caught.

Sophia was the girl I'd lose my virginity to. I grew up with the notion that sex was for marriage. But as our relationship progressed, it felt only right to take it to the next step. Although it was awkward, that first time was special. It meant something. It was two people coming together on the same terms. Sex was everything I thought it would be and should be. But sex later became a tool for self-satisfaction and manipulation. It would get me into precarious situations that would put both my physical and mental health in jeopardy.

Sophia and I would drive around in her two-door Scion late into the night. As the street lights above would flicker like a ticking clock through the sunroof, we'd talk about what would come after graduation. Every kid in my grade would attend a traditional four-year school; it felt like the appropriate path to take. I was excited to graduate and move forward, but I was too busy looking at a possible career and not paying attention to the journey that I was about to set out on. It was naive to think that life would be easy and the answers would settle like a fifty-piece puzzle. Growing up in a bubble made it all seem so black and white. High school prepared me extremely well for college, but not for the realistic challenges of life that awaited.

The last year of high school was an interpersonal journey. I'd sit with my friend Michael on his family's farm, looking at the stars, and wondering what came next. Michael was a kid I grew up with. He had always been an eccentric kid and beat to his own drum. He was into Lincoln Logs and Legos, and liked building shit out of cardboard and duct tape. We certainly had that in common.

As we got into middle and upper school, Michael and I became tied to the hip. We'd play on the JV and varsity football team, although neither of us were good. We stuck together—surviving two-a-days and labs in science class. We had a shared interest in environmental science and went to Charleston on weekend trips to do snail labs.

We were completely oblivious to girls until senior year and did our own thing. Michael was someone I could confide in and talk to about anything. We went to dances but didn't dance with anyone. We played Airsoft in his backyard for hours and went to McDonald's three times in one day. We came out of adolescence to young adulthood together, and that was special.

It was scary to think about life beyond high school. I had grown up in the Country Day bubble and was about to enter the next phase. I was set to attend Film School at NC School of the Arts in Winston-Salem, and the friends that I knew for thirteen years would be splitting off. It was the kind of wonder that was both exciting and scary.

Michael and I did everything by the books. Going to class, getting good grades, going to extracurricular activities, and doing what our parents said. We were good kids who appeared to be ready for what was next. I was only in twelfth grade and already had a youthful nostalgia about my life. I knew what I was good at. I was a passionate creative who was ready to pursue movie-making. But it wouldn't take long before that dream was shattered and the realities of life would crush my ego. It would set off a game of cat and mouse. A game that couldn't be won. A constant chase for the next thrill, the next quick fix.

Sophia would be moving to Ohio to attend Kenyon College. It was a long-distance situation we knew would be difficult, but we agreed to try and make it work. It was a decision that would cause me to lose interest in my own studies and set a pattern of searching for acceptance from other people. I would become a person looking for answers everywhere else but within.

I thought the path would be as clear as the landmarks I grew up seeing on Providence Road. I thought my future would be similar. I grew accustomed to seeing the same things and expecting the same outcomes. But life would tell a different story, taking many branches off the road that defined my youth.

7

Creative Disturbance

We were twenty minutes away from Winston-Salem and the School of the Arts. I was nervous. I didn't know what to expect. *What kind of kids would be there? Where were they from? What was their background with this whole filmmaking thing?* I knew I was creative, but how well would I stack up against the others?

We approached the entrance at the bottom of the hill and followed the signs to the dormitory. It was a three-story brick building with windows that slanted at an angle. It faced a kudzu valley. They were old and had stale energy. My roommate was already there. He was a short guy with long, jet-black hair and glasses who wore fantasy shirts. Not my style, but it was art school; the 'weird' was expected. It was a sharp contrast from the high school setting I just left. We'd get along to start with, but he'd eventually tell me he liked to have sex with dead people. Joking or not, it was fucked up.

The other kids weren't much better. They talked about movies and camera equipment all the fucking time. Apart from the classes I was attending, I preferred to talk about other things. Literally anything else. Classes were long and lasted all day. I'd have general education classes in the morning, then head over to the film buildings for afternoon classes. The film sector was set up like a film set. It was a little bit of Hollywood in the middle of North Carolina. It felt strange and for the first time I wondered what I was doing there. There was something about the contrast between reality and film that I never considered before. It was just another bubble, with my freshman class only having about 130 people. It felt like a parallel high school, but this time around, everyone was the same. I think that was the irony of art school. You tend to think of the art kids as being individuals. The kids that break out. But every kid there just fit the mold of what was expected. It didn't feel like a college experience, and as the weeks went by, I'd question whether I should be there or not.

I'd meet a guy named Jacob. He was from West Virginia and drove a black BMW. His family had made a boatload of money in the coal industry. He was conservative and I found it odd he was at art school. We had an unconscious agreement that we didn't fit in and both of us were love-struck with people who lived far away. We'd bond over how lonely we felt. Jacob and I would drive around Winston-Salem with no particular place in mind, as long as it was anywhere besides campus. We'd patrol Wake Forest in deep regret of where we actually were. School of the Arts wasn't panning into what we both dreamed it would be. It was the first big disappointment of my young adult life and a realization that a dream would soon end.

Bored and depressed as shit, we played basketball against ballerinas and wisecrack about the professors' credentials. The dean wouldn't stop talking about *Fried Green Tomatoes*. He was a producer on the film and still grasped that as his crowning achievement. It was *Fried Green* this, *Fried Green* that. I never saw the movie, but the relentless hounding of its title guaranteed I never would. Movies that I once loved were slowly getting ruined left and right. I didn't even want to go to a theater. It was movie talk 24/7. All I wanted was a break.

I'd go to a few parties around campus, but at that point, I still hadn't picked up a drink. It was a mix of fear and conformity. I didn't want to drink just to fit in. I didn't want that to be my ticket into the social club. But the pressure to fit in would eventually overpower any previous thoughts I had on the matter.

It was a struggle to stay focused on anything besides my long-distance relationship with Sophia. My body was in North Carolina, but my heart was in Ohio. It was a strange feeling of emptiness that I never experienced before. It was innocent naivety that made me believe it could work out. She was my first love, and I wasn't ready to let her go.

I'd make the drive up to Gambier, usually every other weekend, skipping classes regularly. Ever since I was little my

education was one of the most important things in my life. But
now that I found love, going to class didn't seem to matter. I
thought love could solve the problems I was facing in Winston-
Salem. I thought it could mask my loneliness and bring me
purpose. But it only made me question myself more. *Why was I
wasting time at a school I didn't even want to be at?* I thought love
could bridge the gap between expectations and reality.

I put an expectation on myself that film school would meet
my needs. I had an expectation it would grow a passion that
budded only a few years earlier. But I lost track of the purpose of it
all. It was a realization that I wasn't going to become some famous
director in Hollywood. I wasn't going to be some well-known
cinematographer on a film set. It was a reality wake-up call that
adulthood wouldn't progress as easily as I thought it would. Life
was going to be hard, but I thought my love with Sophia would
ease the growing pains. She was one of the few things left from my
past that still had some resemblance of what things had been.

I'd leave school around 7 p.m. on a Thursday and drive
through the night. It was close to 8 hours away and was a lot of
time to sit with my thoughts in a tin can echo chamber. I'd drive
through the rain and snow, looking through the rearview mirror to
a life I wanted to leave behind for good. I'd drive under crystal
blue skies and gray October evenings as the orange sun would roll
under the last set of trees. I'd go through mountain passes and
truck stops and hope my cream-colored sedan didn't break down
from the strains of the road. I'd hope the hole in my tire would
hold out for the next hour and the broken wiper would clear the
bug stains from my windshield. It was a hope and a prayer that
things would work.

I followed my heart and it drove me further from my cold
white brick dorm room at the top of the hill. I remember playing
Delilah on the radio. She'd play audio clips of people whose loved
ones were lost, spouses who died of cancer or in war. It was in
hearing these words of loss when I realized life was more than
going to class and getting a good grade. It was more than making a
dream come true. It was the realization that things don't work out.

49

That life is not fair. There was something about Delilah's voice that was calming. I'd often cry on the ride home knowing I was returning back to Winston-Salem.

My life in Ohio was a far cry from the pain I was feeling back south. I'd spend a lot of time sitting in corn fields and eating free food at the cafeteria. Kenyon was a magical place. Its old Gothic architecture and middle path through the center of campus was something special. It was lined with trees whose colors burned bright at the peak of fall, and the path glistened with softly laid snow in the middle of January. It was the collegiate experience I thought I was missing out on. The campus felt like a real life movie. Students in oversized glasses and thrift store scarfs reading Kurt Vonnegut and talking about ancient philosophy and modern politics. I felt smart just being there. It was a place where Sophia was thriving. It had an energy about it that was far different from mine.

I acted like I was a student there. I'd wear an old green tweed sports coat and a red and white striped scarf that Sophia had bought me. Kenyon became a place where I could be me, but being there was a lie. I didn't go to school there. I could never afford it, let alone get in. My SAT scores sucked. But Sophia always welcomed me with open arms and introduced me to her close-knit group of friends. I think she could see I was struggling, and she tried her best to cheer me up.

Sophia wasn't a drinker in high school, but started once she hit college. It's the story of almost every college freshman. That time when you got too drunk to walk home and pass out in the bushes. That time you made out with too many people to count. It was an experience I had yet to have, but Sophia convinced me otherwise. I said no for so long and finally wanted to just get it out of the way. Part of me wanted to see what all the hype was about. So one evening, I got drunk for the first time in her dorm.

She managed to get hold of a bottle of shit vodka and said she'd take off a piece of clothing for every shot I took. It was a win in my eyes. I'd finally figure out what this whole getting drunk thing was all about and get laid at the same time. I proceeded to drink almost the entire bottle and couldn't get it up.

I liked the feeling. I liked how it made me warm and giggly, how it seemed to open up conversation into areas I wouldn't normally allow. I liked how it seemed to further my connection with Sophia, and that it loosened up my worries. It made me feel comfortable in my own skin. It tasted like shit, but that would be an easy obstacle to overcome. For the first time in my life, I let a foreign substance into my body. It would be the furthest from the last.

I had no idea how that one night would unfold into thousands more and play itself out into an uncontrollable urge that I would chase from sun-up to sun-down. It would open a door with far-stretching hallways leading to substances I never thought I'd try. The game was on.

I stayed for one semester at School of the Arts before moving back home. I skipped too many classes and was disengaged with everything film. I was sick of it. The dream that I started out with just months earlier was gone. Maybe it was the fact that I was always on the road to Ohio, or maybe it was the people at art school whose obsession with film had seemingly pushed me out the door. Maybe it was the film set requirements or the size of each grade? There had been an expectation set by the school that I could not meet.

I felt like a failure on the drive back home. I felt like I let my mom and dad down. I felt confused. What just happened and why was I unable to make it work? This confusion would deepen my depression and further my journey into substance abuse.

It would be demoralizing being back in Charlotte. I would become envious of Sophia's college experience. In fact, all my friends were away having a blast. I had been voted 'most likely to succeed' but felt like an utter failure. What would I do now?

My mom continued to push the importance of an education, encouraging me to enroll at CPCC, the local community college, to complete some core classes. Turns out that was the smartest thing I could have done at the time. Go figure.

They were a third of the price and twice as easy. *Why didn't I do this all along?* I was making some sort of progress, but my undiagnosed depression was getting a lot worse. I continued to drive to Ohio to fill in the missing gaps of my life. The problem was I was simply putting my problems on hold.

CPCC was a melting pot of people and felt the way I imagined college being. There were mothers completing their first degree, single dads, immigrants, first generation college students, and kids fresh out of high school like me. Young and old, we were all there to better ourselves and gain ground in life. It was a completely different population than art school. Not one person was the same. It felt gritty. It felt raw. It was refreshing to see such a diverse palette of personalities and interests.

However, at the same time, community college felt like defeat. Everyone from my high school class was attending name-brand colleges. UNC, Penn, and Harvard, there wasn't one top 10 school left untouched. And here I was, attending the local community college. I'd go to evening classes as my mind wandered to far-off places. It was a mix of jealousy and resentment. Why hadn't the School of the Arts worked out? Had I given up too soon? I'd spend my free time driving around Charlotte like I did only a year earlier.

I was searching for things to take me away from the reality I was living and put my faith in substances to do it for me. I never tried marijuana before and didn't know anyone who sold it. But like any person determined to find an out, I went online and found my calling card. I settled on Spice (this was long before it made it into headline news), a synthetic marijuana that supposedly worked as well as the real deal. I soon had a non-descriptive package in the mail from a sender on eBay. Yes, I bought drugs on eBay.

While my parents were out, I popped open the bag. It looked like dirt and smelled like regret. It was too late to look back. This was bringing some much needed spice (no pun intended) to my seemingly dull and stagnant life. I bought a glass pipe from the local glass shop and Googled how to use it. I was that new to the whole thing. I lit up and breathed in the heavy and harsh smoke. It immediately made my head feel light and I could feel two small weights developing under my eyes. My vision sharpened and my senses were heightened. I could hear the sounds from the smallest insects and the sirens blaring from far-off streets. And the light of the moon sharpened its contrast with the shadows of night. I never felt this way before. It was new and exciting. I spent the next few hours sitting on the porch spinning thoughts around my head. My feelings of loneliness went away and the images in my head became enough to entertain me. I remained still but felt like I was on the move. My imagination became enough to keep my mind enthralled. I was hooked right away.

I'd eventually buy the real thing from my brother, and damn, did it reek. It had a powerful smell that overran my room, making it hard to hide. Weed became a powerful escape from the drudgery of living at home and going to school. I'd smoke before and after class. It seemed to make time go by faster. I'm not totally sure what I was in a rush to do.

Over the course of that semester, I must've driven to Ohio and back at least ten times and it was finally catching up with me. Me and Sophia's lives had naturally grown apart. She was in Ohio creating a community of her own and I was stuck in Charlotte, riding out life, just me and my pipe. She would go to parties while I was sitting in my garage room, and I'd get mad about how drunk she was getting without me. It was pure jealousy and I did my best to ruin any good time she might have.

That summer, we'd both work at a summer camp in Lake George, NY in an effort to find adventure and rekindle our relationship. Although we both hated the job, we'd meet new people, travel to Montreal and Plattsburgh, and get absolutely smashed. It was a last-ditch effort to renew a love that already grew apart. As the summer pulled to a close, she went back to Gambier and I went to Greensboro to try my hand at a new school.

Sophia and I would eventually end after I fucked a girl in the same dorm as me. It was my second stage of 'sexploration' and I was disgustingly proud of myself for having the ability to pull someone other than Sophia. I simply didn't know I had it in me.

And like the first time I drank liquor and smoked a bowl of weed, it opened an aluminum can that couldn't be resealed. The condoms were already out of the bag.

Greensboro was a rundown town and didn't have much to do. I spent most of my days wandering aimlessly around campus or sitting in the empty graphic design lab. I'd meet a couple of frat guys who convinced me to pledge for them after a day of tripping mushrooms. Let's just say, my effort to pledge didn't last long, and I quit after one of the guys stopped me on the way to class. We were told to carry five things at all times; a condom, a lighter, a pack of cigarettes, a bottle opener, and the frat pin—and I had none of them. He told me to get down and do twenty pushups amidst the chaos of students walking by. I hadn't transferred to Greensboro to be someone's bitch and I quit the pledge process on the spot.

I felt embarrassed. Why did I ever think joining such a thing would bring me the connections I so desperately wanted? Sophia was gone, the girl whom I cheated on her with was gone, and the group of guys in the frat house were just another set of macho man wannabees. UNC Greensboro was a college made of commuters and the weekends were isolating. Drinking NyQuil to fall asleep became a daily occurrence. I spent whatever money I had on Bootleggers and shake. I'd wander around campus at night with a buzz and stare at couples walking happily back to their apartments. I'd watch kids in the art building staying late to finish their projects. And I'd eavesdrop as everyone else in the cafeteria talked about last weekend's party as I sat alone spinning around my second helping of melted ice cream. By mid-March I was ready to move on, but didn't know how to go. It was that youthful assumption that every little thing was life and death. I still had classes to finish up and couldn't quit until May. I'd eventually figure a way out, and it came through a girl. Her name was Zoey.

I'd be back in Charlotte for a weekend away from Greensboro and bought tickets to a Ghostland Observatory show for me and my dad. I never heard of them before, but they were playing at my favorite venue, Neighborhood Theater. I had frequented NODA since high school, going to places like the

Evening Muse to watch local musicians. I felt like I belonged in the neighborhood and loved going to Salvador Deli for a soda and sandwich.

We were standing outside the theater prepping our minds the best way I knew how, smoking some bud.

"How'd you get caught?" My dad asked.

He'd gone years undetected by law enforcement apparently. Unfortunately for me, I got caught a few months back with a pipe on UNC Greensboro's campus and was in the middle of a legal nightmare. But after a drug class and several piss tests, it was dropped.

I took the one-hitter and dragged one last time on the harsh smoke. It was surprisingly good weed considering it was my dad's stash. His black-out friend wobbled back and forth. There was no telling what he was on, but looking back on it, I'd guess it was pills.

Standing at the base of the stage was a brown-haired girl in a black leather jacket, black shirt, dark jeans, and a nice pair of shoes. She was the complete opposite of Sophia's preppy style and had a dangerous appeal. Turns out, she wasn't as hardened as she appeared. In fact, she was pretty innocent, but she had style. I'd later find out that Marc Jacobs was her bitch.

She had also grown up in Charlotte. In fact, she went to Charlotte Catholic, the rival of Country Day. Zoey was an identical twin and musically inclined. She played acoustic guitar and spun vinyl records in her room. She had that art side I so dearly loved, but also an innocent side where I could prove how mature I was. She was a virgin, I wasn't. She never smoked weed, I did. She never really drank, that snowball was just starting. She was a girl whom I could show the world to. My world, to be exact.

Ghostland blew me away, but Zoey caught me. She was strikingly beautiful and went to the concert alone. I stood beside her the entire show and eventually mustered up the confidence to ask for her number. On the way back to Greensboro that Sunday afternoon, I thought about her. She went to Appalachian State, a school I previously applied to but was denied entry. I'd spend the rest of that semester driving from Greensboro to Boone planning fun weekends with her in the mountains. We'd go back country camping, spend a snowy weekend in a cabin, and go to parties at my high school friend Michael's house who recently joined a fraternity. She quickly carried my heart to the mountains, and I once again found purpose. It wasn't my studies, it wasn't making new friends, it wasn't my family, it was her. All my focus was on her. It was once again the naive assumption that happiness could be sourced from someone else.

My decision to transfer was finalized. I was tired of driving back to Greensboro sobbing like a child. Tired of sitting in classes I didn't care for. Tired of eating breakfast, lunch and dinner alone. Zoey was a girl I'd do anything for. She had lent me a hand out of Greensboro. With high hopes, I was set to attend Appalachian State, but trouble was just around the corner.

8

Between Rivers and King

I grabbed the dirty mop from the closet and began to pace back and forth alongside the peeling teal booths. There were pepperonis and chunks of dried-up cheese on the worn tiles. It was a shit job at Hungry Howie's, and I had the night shift. When I was a kid, we'd get Hungry Howie's once a week when they had their two-for-one special on Wednesdays. It was one of the few nights my mom decided not to cook. It was cheap pizza, but at that age it tasted especially good. Choosing which flavored crust we wanted was the best part.

I never thought I'd be working there as a young adult, but there I was, answering the phone and manning the cash register. You'd get your typical drunk college kid stumbling in through the doors around eleven or so. My manager was rough around the edges. He had spotted tattoos across his arms, gritty teeth, and a sharp beard. He hired me on the spot; his hiring standards were low. I watched the clock high as shit and sat there drooling with an empty stomach. I don't know if you've ever worked food service on an empty stomach, but it's truly agonizing. The fridge at my apartment was always empty even though my parents would give me a monthly stipend for food. I'd buy a jar of peanut butter and some ramen and call it a meal for a week. All my money went to booze, weed, and whatever other drug I'd stumble across. I'd smoke, get hungry, then drink to fill up. It was an odd cycle.

I clocked out around 12:15 a.m. tired as shit but stepped out into the brisk Boone night ready for a drink. It was never too late to start drinking. It was generally cold on top of the mountain, and a nice glass of brown liquor always seemed to warm me up. It was an excuse to drink at any time of day. Let's blame it on that, am I right?

Riley was at Portofinos. I tended to find her either there or Murphys. She was a short, brown-haired lesbian with big blue eyes. Riley was the kind of person I could call up for anything. She'd do anything for anyone. If I needed a drinking buddy, she was there. If I needed a shoulder to cry on, she was there. I met her through my friend Michael at a frat party he was throwing. He and I had reconnected when I transferred to Appalachian State. He had strangely joined a fraternity, something I thought he'd never do. It was a fraternity full of misfits, not assholes.

Everywhere we went we had to be high, well, I had to be high. This bothered him and he struggled to relate to how far I was taking it. We'd experiment with mushrooms and acid. One night, he and I took a handful of mushrooms and after Sergeant Pepper's Lonely Hearts Club Band came on the stereo, terror completely shook me. I spiraled into a mental white-walled room and couldn't get out. Michael was there, but I couldn't talk to him. My speech was frozen and my body was paralyzed. It was the most terrifying drug trip I ever took. I had gone straight to hell. I swore to never eat mushrooms again, so I turned to acid for my high.

Michael slowed down his drinking while I ramped up mine. This indirectly pushed him further away, and he isolated himself once he moved into a one-bedroom apartment across town. We no longer went on hikes to Hawksbill—one of our favorite spots that he showed me years before, and still one of my favorite spots to this day. We no longer went swimming in the creek or played pool at Boone Saloon. We no longer hung our hammocks on the mall or went to trivia at Gallileos. He no longer wanted to be a part of my life.

It would all come to a head one weekend when we went to his grandparents' mountain house at Grandfather Mountain Country Club. We went there for a weekend snowboarding trip, something I hadn't done since my younger years. I wasn't there to snowboard; I was there to get loaded. We played cards at the dining room table. I hated cards but I loved drinking. Drinking a whole fifth of vodka led to me getting so drunk, I threw up in the downstairs closet and proceeded to piss in it. I didn't give a shit if it was disrespectful and did whatever the hell I wanted.

The next day we woke up early to go to Sugar Mountain. Snow was falling heavily. I was hungover, but still agreed to go. I would later regret that decision. I got off the ski lift at the top of the mountain and sat on the ground making sure my bindings were secure. The world around me was breathing; my head was spinning like a washing machine. I should've stayed at home. I cut down the mountain fast, the tree line distorting into a blur on either side. *How do I stop again*? My brain was mush and completely detached from my body. This wasn't fun. Why the fuck did I agree to this? I hit a patch of ice and slammed to the ground, bashing my elbow. It hurt like hell and I sat up on my ass, throwing up yellow bile multiple times. I cursed to God and then to myself. I just wanted to go home. I slid the rest of the way down the mountain and was driven home by Michael. That was the end of my trip.

The ski trip was the last drop in the bucket for Michael. He grew tired of my antics. It was the inevitable ending point to a friendship that had begun cracking long before. Michael and I went from best friends to total enemies. He wanted nothing to do with me and all productive conversation was out the window. He was no longer interested in my goals and dreams because, well, I didn't have any.

I thought of my friends like a revolving door—some stayed longer than others and others simply gave up on the ties that once bound us. Most had been mere acquaintances—people I saw out on the town or at the houses I bought drugs from.

As fast as I was to fall in love, I was equally as fast to give up on friendships. I cared about them as long as my glass permitted. And as I got older, my friend group got smaller, eventually just becoming me.

But during that time in Boone, Riley and I were bound at the hip. We immediately connected over a game of flip cup and spent the rest of the night drinking as many Pabst Blue Ribbons as we could. She was a small girl but damn she could drink. We'd smoke a bowl before class and get completely lit the night before 'syllabus day.' That was the name we gave to the first day of class when all we did was skim over a syllabus and skip out early. Riley was the friend I could count on during those long winter days where Boone shut down under feet of snow. She'd stay up until the early morning hours long after the last person passed out next to their empty Burnett's bottle. Boone was a small town and meeting someone at a bar and partying with them late into the night was normal. It was a safe town and I rarely had apprehensions about the people I'd meet. Granted, I was usually off my rocker and filled with booze.

Portofinos was a bar along Rivers Street that hung over Boone Creek. It was right next to Jimmy Smith park, the world's smallest public green space, and had a porch that extended onto the parking lot. Like all other bars in Boone, it had shit food, but a precarious setting: a pool table under a fluorescent light bulb and dusty shelves with low grade liquor. I got to Portofinos that night, worn out but ready to drink. I was always ready to drink. Riley was my best friend, and we stuck together like a flame to a glass pipe. I passed Riley and a group of her lesbian friends and made my way to the back of the bar where the pool tables and darts were. Riley was busy, so I decided to play an older man who was already playing solo. I wasn't very good at either, but it was always a good carrot for conversation. The man had a Goodwill-type look, not all that odd for the area, with dark greasy hair and a clean-shaven face. He looked a bit rough, but who was I to judge? I didn't look much cleaner.

He agreed and we played until closing time. By that time Riley had already gone home, and I was drunk and alone. There were many nights before where we showed up together and left separately, so Riley wasn't worried this time around. Me and the man were engaged in good conversation, so in my clouded mind, I invited the man back to my apartment to have a nightcap. I barely remember the next three days.

He came home that night with me with the cruelest intentions; I can see that now. I have flashes of standing in the small kitchen pouring drinks, him taking off his clothes, then him taking off mine and laying in bed. He had slipped a drug into my drinks at the bar and again at my apartment and forced himself on top of me, driving me to perform God knows what. I was in no state of mind to stop him and was out cold on date drugs. The next morning is also a series of scattered memory flashes.

He borrowed my car to get his things from the rag-tag motel up the road and was under the impression he was moving in. I was blinking in and out of consciousness and had no problem with it. Riley later told me she stopped by that morning to smoke a bowl before heading to class and met the man. She said she was scared for me but didn't say anything, because for all she knew, I was okay with it. I remember bits and pieces of going to my math lab, talking to my partner and very quickly leaving, after she asked, "Are you okay?"

When I got home from the math lab, the man was still there. Piles of music tapes and an old 80's boombox littered the room. There were unfolded clothes cast around the floor and a trash bag filled with canned food. He gave me another drink, and the confusion continued. It was like I could tell something was wrong but couldn't form the words to tell him to get out. My friend Aiden would see me that afternoon sitting outside my apartment in the bushes staring into space. He called out to me, but I didn't respond. I was gone.

A few hours later, the man's friend came by. He had just gotten out of the Watauga County jail, and I invited him in with open arms, my brain completely detached from my consciousness. My friend Wyatt came by that evening and met both characters. I believe his response was, "What the fuck?" Internally I was gone, but I appeared to be okay on the outside. I was making dangerous decisions without even knowing it. That night was a repeat of the previous one.

All three friends who saw me that day later told me they were concerned for my safety. They knew, though, if they said anything, I wouldn't have listened. By that point, I was well down the road of drug addiction and alcoholism. Whatever you thought, you were wrong. I didn't listen to anyone. I was unapologetically selfish but thought I got what I deserved. Everything leading up to that moment was a cause of my decisions. I was a broken person who expected broken things. I was a person whose respect for their body and safety became secondary.

That third morning, I snapped awake. The melted room solidified into recognition, and I once again saw myself in the mirror. The murky haze over my eyes cleared, and I could finally walk straight. My clothes were sticky and disgusting, and my hair was slicked back with grease. *What the hell happened and who the fuck was this dude?* I woke up yelling at the man and demanded he get out immediately. He tried to talk me down, but I threw his shit out the door and closed it behind him. I fell to the floor and broke down in tears. *What had just happened to me?* I was embarrassed. Embarrassed enough to not say anything to anyone. My body was used and discarded, and I felt like filth. In an effort to make myself better, I went to the liquor store and bought a bottle. It would be a habitual pattern of covering up for the previous day's decisions. Those two nights changed me forever because I would continue to use my own body as a dumping ground of abuse.

The addiction process had begun and would build slowly over the following years. I'd spend my last dollar on booze. No one stopped me because they were doing the same. There was only one liquor store, and you could usually find me there between noon and 5 p.m.; I had a break between classes then. I'd buy a flavored Burnett's fifth and some soda. My taste buds were shot, and I lived off the bottle and Cookout. Neither filled me up. It was normal to stay out until three in the morning. The thought of school was always on the back burner, and my projects were always done last minute.

Riley and I would drive drunk up to Howard's Knob and smoke a bowl on its overlook just because we could. There was an abandoned black house just before the entrance that was full of mystery. I mean, this place was huge and had a big red dot on its exterior that faced down on campus. There were rumors that a distasteful professor threw sex parties within its walls. Or maybe it was an old grow house. Neither would surprise me. Boone was a place full of debauchery. It was a place where people drank more than they studied. It seemed normal to drop acid on a Tuesday, slip

62

into a "K-hole" before happy hour, smoke DMT before studying, or ride a unicycle to class. There was a kid who carried a boom box everywhere. There were many who didn't wear shoes. I mean we're talking real hippie shit. Ironically, they still ate McDonald's.

Sanford Mall was full of hammocks, slack lines and ultimate frisbee. If you didn't have Chacos or wear Patagonia, who were you? I often found myself on the fringes. I didn't connect with anyone in Wey (the art building). I came and went after every studio class and half-assed almost all my projects. I was either high or drunk. Actually, I was both. I'd snort lines of coke before heading to my art education classes and take a bathroom break to finish off the bag in my pocket. My days were consumed with finding the next high. Whether through women, drugs, or alcohol, it didn't matter. If I wanted it, I was out to get it and it didn't matter who was going to get hurt.

The more time I spent amongst my peers, the more I distanced myself from the art I was creating. I usually dragged in a minute or two after class started, hungover from the night before. I'd take out my newsprint and charcoal and stare at naked drama kids striking poses on the professor's call. They got paid minimum wage to strut their stuff. There wasn't much to see.

My first apartment was tucked away behind the Klondike Bar, a place where sorority girls and frats guys groped one another or picked sissy fights between rival houses. I went there a few times but didn't fit in. It didn't matter, though. There were other watering holes.

There was a good view outside my kitchen window. I'd stand there in the morning and look out upon campus or watch a storm sweep in from over the hill. You could always see it coming but still braced for its impact. I spent a lot of time there alone, especially during breaks when most students went home. I'd line up vodka bottles on top of the cabinets like some sort of fucked-up trophy parade and collect glass smoking pipes like I was running an opium den. It was an apartment that became the breeding ground for my habits. Habits that would come close to killing me many times over.

I had my twenty-first birthday there, and like any other amateur drinker, I blacked out and woke up the next morning, calling it a success. Zoey and I had broken up after a series of drunken fights and we fell out of love. I think we both realized it became more of a friendship, and the temptations walking around campus were too much for the both of us. There were no hard feelings even after she frantically stormed to my apartment one afternoon and accused me of giving her an STD.

"It was probably that bartender at Boone Saloon you've been fucking," I said.

I knew it wasn't me. Up to that point, I avoided all venereal diseases. Surprisingly, we remained friends for some time after the breakup.

I'd spend my free time as a single person going all in, literally. I'd run through a series of women with zero regard for human empathy and love. It was all about what I wanted and whatever emptiness left by Zoey would be filled by the next person I'd come across.

I'd meet a cute girl named Everly a month and a half after Zoey and I broke up. She was a freshman whom I met in the cafeteria. She was from Charlotte and looked to me for a good time. I tried my best to give it to her the only way I knew how. I supplied her with alcohol, and she supplied me with sex. There were no labels; it seemed like a good enough situation to pass the time, and we got along well. She was a sorority girl and dragged me to an event in Blowing Rock one evening. I had nothing better to do—my motivation was that there'd be free alcohol. The guys at the event felt pride in the fraternities in which they resided. They had a group of people with seemingly similar values and girls that fit the bill. They had solidarity in something, something that gave them purpose, no matter how stupid it might have been. Even if all they did was hold secret meetings and pay for friends, it still was something. Having a solid group of people was something I craved and had yet to find, but I knew it wouldn't be there. Everly's world would clash with mine, and we ended soon after.

Following Everly there seemed to be a flurry of short flings. It was a never-ending cycle of going out at night, meeting someone new, getting crazy drunk, and smashing each other. I often found my emotions overriding common sense. I'd get intertwined with people I really didn't care for, but I'd still fall hard—at least until I didn't. That was the Pisces in me. I was a walking contradiction who said one thing and did another. I knew it wasn't right but did it anyway. This type of cycle would continue to define my habits beyond the dating scene.

That first summer in Boone I'd meet a girl named Claire. She was a person I'd see just to say I had someone. By that point it felt strange to sleep alone. It's funny who you go out with in desperation. Looking back, we really had nothing in common. I'd meet her at Boone Saloon on a weekday afternoon. She was vegan, tatted, and super skinny: the hipster trifecta. We'd walk to Earth Fare, and she'd buy a pack of soy nuggets that cost more than what I'd eat for three days. She also had a small white dog that I dragged on a hike to the top of Grandfather Mountain. That little shit wasn't even winded.

Amongst all the seasonal flings, my group of guy friends stayed consistent. Wyatt was one of those guys. He was the most level-headed person out of all of them. He grew up in Kernersville and had a simple approach to life. He was practical, steady. Out of every guy I hung out with, he's the one who kept the straight and narrow. I mean, we got loaded, but it always had an ending point for him. He knew when to call it quits. We'd spend a lot of time together talking about if this, college, was it. He had dreams of going to Thailand, which he eventually did. Although I wanted to join him in this endeavor, it would be impossible due to my addiction.

Wyatt would comfort me with his words day after day, and I eventually grew to understand that he wasn't there to get drunk and high. He was there for me, the person I was under the rough, bruised skin. He was one of the few that cared deeply about the person I could be, not the person I was.

65

One night, Wyatt and I were sitting on my porch. We had just gotten home from the bar, and it was late. I had eaten a handful of mushrooms an hour earlier, and they were beginning to kick in. Notice it was just me who ate them? This was nothing out of the ordinary. We sat chatting about cloud formations and post-graduation goals when Claire came out, dropped her panties and took a piss next to our fold out lawn chairs. She was sleepwalking and proceeded to walk inside. Wyatt and I turned to each other with a synchronous, "Did that just happen?!" expression.

Claire became a little too needy for me after she asked me to look after her dog multiple times while she went to work. Claire and I didn't last much longer, and without even considering the consequences I told her I had HIV. Why in God's name I thought that was a good way out, I will never know, but it was the best excuse I could come up with. You can imagine how well that went over and a week later I told her it was a lie.

Crazy seemed to follow me everywhere. I'd get evicted from my apartment two weeks before I was leaving for a study abroad program in Sweden. I woke up to a half-inch of water, solo cups and half-smoked cigarettes throughout my apartment, and my landlord standing in the doorway calling out my name. Apparently, the trash barrel that was holding the keg had a hole in it. The night before was a blur full of beer pong, bong smoke, and Ketamine. I threw a few traffic cones off the balcony and my clothes were wet. Neighbors complained, but I didn't care. It must have been the graduate student on the first floor. I made the Gray Squirrel Apartments my bitch, and I bowed out the best way I knew how.

I lived in one other place in Boone. It was behind Jimmy Johns, adjacent to the business building. It was a strange place with an entrance that led to a slender room straight into a tiny kitchen. The bedroom faced an alley. It had poison ivy across a shitty patch of land out front, a fitting display that matched the building's name, Ivy Hall. I'd get poison ivy on multiple occasions and eventually got it on my dick, which swelled up like a reverse cone. It was an unsavory place whose landlord did the bare minimum to keep it up, and it would be the place where my body would be thrown into disarray on countless occasions.

I'd leave the window open and blast the band Tennis through a speaker intended for Legends Theater, the local music venue. Surprisingly, my neighbors never complained. I had an open-door policy, inspired by Warhol's Factory, that brought in both familiar and strange characters. I started out with furniture, but all of that was eventually destroyed by my friend Wyatt after I encouraged him after a night of drinking.

My place was full of powder. My buddy drove down to Atlanta where he bought a half ounce of blow. We all said that we'd divide it up and sell it, but my share ended up sitting above the fridge in a Beatles lunch box. It didn't last long. It didn't matter whether I was going to class or going to the library to study. At the last minute, that shit went up my nose. My neighbor, Jayden, always had the party favors. He was someone I met out of chance. I had just gotten back from a road trip to Canada and was tired from the sixteen-hour drive. It was a school holiday, and I pulled into my apartment ready to smoke a bowl and go to sleep. However, my neighbor had other plans. He just got out of the Boone jail due to another DUI and approached me as I was outside smoking a cigarette. His hair was a mess and his wire glasses lay slanted on his sweaty face. He asked if I wanted to come over for a beer. I was tired but agreed. The decision to invite him into my life would forever change who I was. A few weeks later, he was dropping LSD onto my tongue, passing me handfuls of Xanax and showing me the Monterey Pop documentary he had on TV.

Jayden was a business major and had transferred schools several times—we had that in common. He was a heavy drug user, way more than me, but he took me under his wing and showed me I was merely an amateur. He would drag around a nitrous oxide tank and invite me to take balloons. He'd fish out on the floor in front of me. It looked like he was having a seizure, and I did nothing to help him. He said he was okay.

We'd waste a lot of time at Ivy Hall. I'd sit in his room as he'd pull out pill bottle after pill bottle from his bedroom, and we'd eat them like candy. He had been to rehab before, but obviously it didn't work. Characters would stroll in after class or from the street and beg for a free hit. Many times, I'd walk by and there'd be people queued outside, waiting for him to get home. I'd spend a lot of all-nighters there, not studying, but high as a kite. Looking back, those nights were pointless. We were literally the masters of nothing.

Jayden and I would continue to hang out until my graduation. I walked into his whirlwind willingly but became trapped. We'd use heroin, nod off or get sick to our stomach. We'd take ecstasy to go play pool, which looking back now, makes no sense. It all seemed normal, or at least harmless, while I was in it. That's the funny part about using drugs: abnormal becomes normal. Your perception of the world increasingly becomes truthful reality, pushing others' reality to the side.

Jayden was a smart guy; most drug addicts are. Jayden was charismatic; most drug addicts are. Jayden was a ladies' man; most drug addicts are. Jayden was lost; most drug addicts are. Our friendship was defined by drug use, but even that became tainted and the colorful nights dulled.

A few months after I moved into Ivy Hall, I met a girl named Haley. She was a music major with dark features and pale skin. She had a presence about her that reflected a rough past, but it fit my present. We connected immediately over a few drinks. She was innocent, and I was wild. We'd stay up late drinking cheap beer and fuck each other until one of us tired. She conveniently lived behind me and would stumble home in an oversized t-shirt before class. We spent a lot of time together, and we'd come in and out of each other's lives for years to come. It was a strange relationship where we didn't say, 'I love you,' but cared for each other in unspoken ways. It was a relationship that would eventually drive me to move to Nashville.

One night I told her I was going to buy a pizza. Lies— I was getting used to telling them. Instead, I bought heroin outside of the Golden Corral in the Walmart parking lot. Haley found out once we got home. To my surprise, it didn't phase her. I figured, score. I blew down a line and proceeded to throw up in my dirty toilet. This happened six more times that month. Haley wasn't into drugs that much at the time, but she let me have free reign. It probably scared her enough to not say anything.

The binges continued and drinking, smoking, and tripping became a nightly occurrence. It was a habitual pattern of physical and mental tests. I was frying my brain slowly but steadily. I'd take Oxycontin, drink a fifth of vodka, and smoke a few bowls before eventually collapsing in the bathroom and whacking my face on the side of the toilet. I proceeded to throw up on myself and got shingles. The next day I laid on my bed, paralyzed from the neck down. I definitely had alcohol poisoning, and no one was there to help me. But that was okay, it was all on me and I deserved it. No one forced me to do it.

Haley would later tell me she walked in that night and saw me. She checked my breathing to see if I was dead, realized I wasn't, and soon left. To any other person, this would be alarming, but I brushed it off as true love. Love for me was anyone who would go along with my antics. Anyone who would ignore my problems enough to not say anything. And anyone who would wake up with me the next day and watch me do it all again.

During the summer I'd go to local swimming spots such as Boone Beach, snake pit, and a secret spot just past the two-story wooden hotel and gas station. It was a sharp right and a place defined by personality. I'd meet my friends there almost every weekend during the summer. We'd make fires on the sand and wade out in the shallow creek to the big gray rocks basking in the sun.

Shit went down there. I'd take my friend's car home without permission while he and his girlfriend were passed out on the beach. Drunk and blacked out, I have no idea how I drove home safely. He later got back at me by fucking his girlfriend on my bed while I was at the bar. By open door policy, I didn't mean that, but I guess I deserved it. The two-story wooden hotel would later burn down.

We'd sit on my neighbor's tin roof and listen to the marching band practicing at the nearby stadium. I'd sit there as he played 'No Rain' by Blind Melon on the guitar for the hundredth time, and we tried our best to rap over instrumental beats we found on YouTube. Summer days were often boring, and we eventually ran out of things to do by mid-July.

I'd work a summer gig at the Linville Country Club, waiting tables and hanging out with a girl named Samantha. She was an attractive blonde-haired girl with curves that fit her bathing suit well. Like many before her, she enjoyed my wild side. We spent the summer in a drunken haze and stayed up all night. I was only taking two summer school classes, but other than those, neither of us had any real responsibilities. Summer classes were popular with students because they were the nicest months to be in the mountains. That type of weather didn't last long, and fall would come fast followed by a long winter. Samantha would eventually leave once her frat-tastic boyfriend returned for the fall semester. I had no idea she had a boyfriend the entire time and felt used. I guess that beach trip we took with my family meant nothing.

I was tired of struggling but had a sudden influx of cash provided from the student loan I took out to pay for my fifth year of college. I blew through two thousand dollars in less than two weeks, buying an ounce of weed, bags of cocaine, couture glass pipes, shots for the bar and liters of high-class liquor. My parents would eventually call me and ask if I received the loan. I told them the truth and crumbled with shame and guilt. If my dad didn't stop me, I would've blown it all.

I eventually got tired of my situation in Boone. Classes were dragging on, and I was constantly broke from blowing my money on whatever I could find. I tried to sell art I made along King Street, but only made twenty dollars. Half of that profit came from my friend, Aiden, who was a supporter of the things I made. I'd scrounge up change from the floorboard of my car, only to spend it on two-dollar Four Loko. That shit was gross, but it did the trick.

I'd sneak into my neighbor's apartment and take a frozen meal or two. His door was always unlocked, and I went up there a few times to fill my belly. He'd lend me his old iPad to play music; I sold it on Craigslist to make a hundred dollars. I was a selfish prick only concerned with getting my next high.

Everyone around me struggled; money, addiction, class, or a combination of the three. But I assumed this was what the college experience was all about. Things were supposed to be messy.

I'd eventually feel the creeping essence of adulthood close behind me. It was time to shed my reckless ways and put on the suit of professionalism. The only problem was, I didn't know how. The mountains had lost their grandeur. I simply wanted to graduate. My apartment had graffiti on every wall and even on the fridge. The place looked like a crack house. My parents would come visit me a few weeks before graduation and were absolutely horrified. I'd later find out that my mother bawled the entire ride home. She thought my behavior would be a phase, but my time in Boone was just the beginning.

I was tired. I would wake up after hosting a party to a completely trashed house. The start of a new day only meant trying to heave my crumbling self up for another one. The only things that consistently kept me company were the memories of drunken people and fuzzy speech ringing in my ear. I was suspended in the past, not caring about the present or future.

Graduation day was a gray event. It didn't feel like success. I didn't feel like I accomplished anything. I exhaled orange but inhaled blue. I didn't have a plan. I was moving back home to Charlotte, where I would complete my student teaching.

I walked down the aisle in my cap and gown, happy faces surrounding me. Other graduates decorated their caps while I just opened my stiff gown from the plastic wrap an hour before. I was hungover and my eyes were stationed on the big screen that read the graduates' names. *What if I got up there and my name didn't appear?* It wouldn't surprise me. I was a ragged dog being pulled by the chain of time.

I took my diploma and wondered, what now? My parents were happy with relief. I let them down many times before, and they always thought this day would be a turning point. I stepped out into the cold December rain in my wrinkled gown. I was surprised it wasn't snowing. Watching over the town that did so well at tearing me down, I walked down the stairs and made the turn to my car, my sister not far behind me. I was glad she could see this accomplishment, but what she didn't see was how broken I felt on the inside. I couldn't share how I felt because I didn't want to hurt her. I was her older brother and didn't want to let her down. And I didn't look back.

9

Latitude and Longitude

I always wanted to travel on my own. It was this inner youthful bug that decided things were better in a distant place. It was the belief that if I could just go somewhere else, my problems would be gone. That my thoughts would get stuck in the thick forests of the mountains and addictions would drown in the cold streams. That my problems wouldn't follow me at thirty thousand feet. Well, that wishful thinking would be proven wrong in time.

I always wanted to study abroad and was finally able to do so when I was 21. Looking back, I'm surprised I made it home alive. I moved to a small college town in south Sweden in early September, 2011. I went alone. I was nervous, but also excited about who I may meet and where I would go. Linnaeus University was a clash of the old and the new, Gothic architecture alongside IKEA furniture. There was an old castle on the banks of the lake. The campus was big and had a large mix of both domestic and foreign students. It was a nice blend of people, and I was surprised to see how well they all spoke English. That made it easier to live, except for the supermarket, where I bought products based on the picture on the label. There were only a few Americans there. One was from Florida, the other two were from New York City and Boston. The Swedes knew the Hollywood cities but had never heard of Charlotte. I liked the ambiguity of it and felt like I could be anyone. I definitely took advantage of that notion.

I roamed around campus with students from France, Belgium, Poland, Canada, and Japan. We got along well, partly because we couldn't understand half of what we were saying to one another, but mostly because we liked to get fucked up together. We went to Copenhagen a lot because it was only a two-hour train ride south. Out of all the places I went, Copenhagen was the most enticing. It's a place I still say I could live in to this day. Everyone rides bikes there, a farfetched idea here in the states.

There was this tiki bar we found on our first trip there that sold 20 shots for 20 kronor, or about $25 U.S. dollars. And let me tell you, we got lit. We'd go to Christiania, a hippie commune in the middle of the city, buy pre-rolled joints and smoke them by the river. We'd walk around Tivoli and look at the giant tower that swung you around on swings. We'd sit at the cafes and drink Irish Coffee and smoke cigarettes. I felt like I fit in.

While on campus, I'd go to Slottsstallarna, a college club on campus, and dance until I ran out of money, and at one of those parties, I met a short Albanian girl named Adriel. Her family moved to Sweden to escape the Albanian War. She worked as a translator and dreamed about moving to New York City. She knew four languages and seemed cultured. She'd stay over at night, and the next morning, we'd go to breakfast at the cafeteria and listen to the Tallest Man on Earth over the speaker. It felt like a strange dream that came true. I always wanted to date a foreign girl, and it was happening just a month into being abroad. I think by now you can see a pattern in where my priorities were.

I became attached, just like I did many times before, and we traveled to Berlin for a week to visit a friend of hers. He was a hip German who was in a band and lived in East Berlin. We stayed in his loft and smoked weed and cigarettes into the early morning. The sound of the shop gates opening told us to go to sleep. Berlin was an artistic paradise. Street art was everywhere, and gypsies and vagabonds roamed without a care; they were present and happy where they were. They were them. We'd go to a three-day rave at an old WWII factory where I'd buy acid from a stranger and wander home with Adriel under the yellow metros reaching their last stop. We slept on the floor the entire time. It was comfortable being in a place unknown. Catching z's wasn't my priority. We'd go to the Berlin Wall and see where the city had once been divided. The history of the city was addicting.

On the train ride home, the script flipped. I was about halfway done with my stint in Sweden and the days were becoming shorter. The sun would rise around 3pm and set around 6pm. There were many days when I barely caught the sun and would roll out of bed to get to my furniture design class around 6:30 p.m. They were interesting classes but easy as hell. I guess the expectations were low for foreign students. My mind just wasn't focused on school; it was hooked on Adriel. Looking back, that wasn't the right priority, and I was honestly lost. I was continually trying to find happiness from external factors. But nothing would help my wandering ways.

By this point, the snow was falling on campus for a while and the white was building up around me. It was pretty, but I saw it so much before. It brought on an odd feeling of bad nostalgia and reminded me of the dark lonely times when I would walk King Street in Boone with no destination in mind. I thought going to Sweden would be life-changing, but life only followed me there. I was the same person in a different setting. I still had the same depression, the same thoughts that rose with the sun and drowned in the dusk. The same empty wallet, the same half-assed friendships and the same destructive habits. But it felt more acceptable to do what I was doing. I was the fun American who had beer pong tournaments in his apartment and the crazy kid who bought hash from the sketchy Swedish drug dealer on campus. It was the same shit, just in a different place. I wasn't sure when I'd be back, if ever. I wanted more in the things I couldn't see. There was something else out there. Adriel was gone, and I was upset with myself for putting all my time into her. There were so many other people around to have fun with.

Thanksgiving passed with me sharing a pepperoni pizza with my buddy, Christian, from Canada. He was a short guy, with a black stubble beard, who loved sports and hitting on women just about as much as me. We were two young adults who connected over finding adventure. We spent that Thanksgiving watching the NFL games that were bootlegged through some sketchy site. I was beginning to miss home but felt like I hadn't taken full advantage of my time there. I hadn't explored enough countries, met enough people, and gotten into enough hairy situations. I craved adventure. In mid-December, Christian and I decided to spend the remaining weeks we had jet setting around Europe.

Our first stop was Barcelona. We stayed in a hostel at the end of the beach and went to the clubs down the way. We had no plans, at least none to see any history, at least. We were hell-bent on making our own history. The beach was crawling with Moroccans that sold hash, and we couldn't resist. We didn't worry about getting arrested. We rolled small spliffs and roamed around the beach the first day and stayed out late trying our best to flirt with women in sign language.

On our second night out we met a Spanish guy who was around our age that offered us an invitation to his place. We figured, score. We had made it a goal to mix in with the locals as much as possible. The three of us took the subway to the outskirts of the city and entered a dark warehouse with burning trash cans. This wasn't the type of flat I was imagining. It looked like a homeless camp, but being the stupid adventurers we were, we sat around the fire with the stranger and two of his friends that showed up. They poured us a drink, but I didn't have any. I had flashbacks to what happened back in Boone. But Christian drank one, then two, then three. I was faded, but one of us had to be coherent enough if shit hit the fan. After an hour or so, two of the men left the room. Christian began to fade in and out, and my heartbeat paced harder as my palms got sweaty. I was starting to get nervous. I had no idea where we were. It was a stupid idea to go there, and the guy said he was going to get more booze. I looked over at Christian who, by this point, looked something beyond drunk. He looked drugged. We looked at each other in sudden sobriety and quickly got up to leave, with Christian struggling to walk in a straight line. We didn't want to see what might happen once the guy or his friends got back. We stumbled out into the moonlight and crept through a half-fallen chain link fence into an empty street. It was an industrial area and it was after hours. It took us four hours to walk home that night. We had no idea where we were.

We woke up the next morning and laughed at the situation. *What the hell just happened?* We shrugged it off with a smirk and a sign of good luck, so we bought cocaine from a shady character on the beach that afternoon and blew it up our nose before we went out. We're lucky he wasn't a cop.

I ended our last night in Barcelona with a female expat from France and woke up in a panic at 2 p.m. to catch my flight to Lisbon at 5 p.m. I had no idea where I was, but knew I was butt-naked. I quietly rolled out the front door as she slept. I didn't remember her name and it didn't matter.

I made my way to the subway station in a confusing effort to find the hostel. I bailed on Christian earlier that night and didn't know if he made it home. I later found out he jumped a cab after realizing he didn't have any money. Apparently, the cab driver chased after him but he got away. We got on the bus and made our way to the airport, passing by all the tourist traps that we purposefully had missed. It didn't feel right to miss such important landmarks, but this wasn't a Rick Steve's best sights to see; it was a drug-fueled adventure to see who could get the most fucked up.

Halfway to the airport Christian realized he forgot his passport and wallet at the hostel and in a split-second jumped off the bus, leaving me on it. Thirty minutes later I got to the terminal, and five minutes later I realized it was the wrong one. There was no way I was going to make this flight. I jumped back on the bus and got off at the right terminal with ten minutes to spare. The situation would have given anyone else a panic attack, but I took it as a sign of pride. I was always able to get out of hairy situations. To my surprise, Christian was already in line waiting. We were on our way to Lisbon.

We knew Lisbon's drug laws were loose and that was mostly the reason we went there. We arrived at a rickety hostel on a large, slanted hill and passed out as we arrived late. It was Christmas Eve, and Christian and I sat in our room, lonely. I think we missed our families. This would be the first time I would spend Christmas away from what I knew. The hostel had some makeshift Christmas decorations in the lobby, and we made friends with the night shift worker behind the counter. He was around our age. We struck up a conversation, and he offered to get us some LSD. He said it was some of the best he knew, so we figured why not. He came back and handed us the doses. We decided to eat it once everyone had gone to sleep.

We dosed in the room and could feel it coming on, making our way to the social room and sitting on the floor in front of a mediocre red Christmas tree. The guy behind the counter offered to look after us. It was a lot of faith to put in a stranger, but he seemed nice enough. Christian never tried acid before, so I wasn't sure how he would react. It came on strong, and the ceiling above me started to flow like a river. The television was playing some sort of French language music video, and the red tree started to pulse. I was lost in the jingle bells of thought. *Where was Santa Claus?* I used to track him online, but now I was on his sleigh. There wouldn't be presents to open in the morning, but it seemed like I was finding them in the patterned rug I was sitting on. The thought of Santa riding around on a magic carpet sprinkling fairy dust on lucky kids cracked us up. Christian was crawling around the carpet like a baby and had a giant grin on this face. His brain was melting.

It's a good thing no other guests came down. Christian and I decided to venture back up to the room. We were still tripping hard. The sun was rising above the sea and the birds came alive. 'Like a Rolling Stone' by Bob Dylan came on the player, and it felt like Bob was sitting outside our window. The sound of his music felt like home, and all of a sudden, Christmas came to us. Bob was the gift, I assumed. But that feeling soon faded, and we were lower than dog shit on a sidewalk. The high had worn off, but our next location offered a continuation. We wasted the last day sleeping the drugs off, then hopped on the bus back to the airport. It was like we were never there.

We arrived in Amsterdam continuing our fucked-up, drug-fueled odyssey. The air was thick with the comforting smell of weed and we made our first stop—a coffee shop. Next on the agenda was the mushroom shop. We had to get our arsenal ready for the night. We walked past the Anne Frank house where the line wound around the corner. We weren't there to see a little girl trapped, for we were trapped inside our own minds. We got back to the hostel where two Brazilian dudes were staying on the bunks next to us. We took the shrooms out and I ate the whole box, completely disregarding the nightmarish trip I had taken just a year before in Boone. The recommendation was four or five, but I took about twenty. We were in Amsterdam after all, why not go balls deep? We played pool downstairs for an hour or so and walked to another coffee shop to relax. Old, worn-out men and tourists filled the dark corners and for a minute, I felt like a poet. In reality, I was seeing double, not writing haikus.

We then decided to go to the Red Light District with the dirtiest intentions. By this point in the trip, whatever morals we had left had flown out the window. It didn't cross my mind on whether it was right or wrong, whether the girls were a part of a sex trade, or whether or not the prostitute was getting any of the cut. I was there just to say I did it. It was probably one of the worst excuses I could come up with, but it worked for me at the time.

I picked one of the girls from a window, like picking a winter coat that didn't fit. The girl looked like a straight up porn star, which when I think about it, isn't that attractive. I won't go into details, but it was done in twenty minutes and was surprisingly clean. I didn't bring back any permanent souvenirs.

We left Amsterdam and made a few more stops in Antwerp, Brugge, and rang in the new year in Brussels at my buddy Jean's house, whom I met in Sweden. The new year was nothing particularly special, just a blurred-out dance floor and throwing up in the sink.

We got back to Sweden to cold ground, worn paths, and a few more weeks to spare. The lake where I threw several bikes into one night was frozen over. The regret hadn't melted. The clubs on campus were no longer interesting. The apartment I was staying in seemed smaller. I bought a few more grams of hash from the campus dealer to smoke out the rest of my days there. I would walk out into the countryside on moonlit nights, away from anyone who could smell it. I struggled with the lighter as the wind blew out my flame. The nights were long and the days were short. I was ready to go home. I planned on leaving without paying the dealer back, but he paid me a visit with two large Norwegians and walked me to the ATM. I couldn't get away with it. That was the icing on the cake. Who else had I screwed over there, and who was waiting for me back in the States?

I went to Sweden to find an adventure and found it in some ways. But I also felt like I wasted my time. The people whom I met, I would probably never see again, and the person I thought I loved really meant nothing. Those airplane rides to other countries were lost on me while the information from the classes I took didn't soak in. I flew to Sweden by myself to find myself, but it felt like I was only bringing home more baggage. The problems I fled were only waiting for me and would only get bigger upon my return. I was still the same person who had stepped on the airplane and said goodbye to my parents. I was still the same person who lied to peoples' faces and drained everything I could from them for my advantage. I was still an alcoholic and drug addict who was in denial. The latitude and longitude made no difference.

I looked back on Sweden with regret. I looked back on a boy that took advantage of people and his situation. I looked back on a kid who only fed himself. I looked back and understood why I was sitting where I was that day.

10

Considering Options

When I got back home to Charlotte following my graduation from Appalachian State, I was more deflated than the popped balloons on the gymnasium floor. I walked to the bedroom I'd be staying in and passed out. I was up the whole night before drinking and barely made it to the ceremony. As I laid in bed, I stared at the ceiling and let the memories wash over my cold and beaten body. The past few years were mostly a secret affair. My mom, dad, brother, and sister had little knowledge of the real happenings. I knew some secrets would be too hard to forgive. I had lied, stolen, and secluded myself from all things family. I had a fast-developing drug and alcohol problem that my mom would soon try and wish away. Who I thought I was and who my parents thought I was were two completely different things. The skeletons in my closet weren't ready for judgment.

I woke up a few hours later to a small gathering of close family friends namely, Brian, Terri, and their son, Hayden. Brian and Terri were like second parents to me growing up.

I always viewed Hayden as my little brother, and felt in some ways, it was my responsibility to show him the ropes. Hayden had spotted freckles across his face, glasses that would often slide off the tip of his nose, a buzzcut, and a high-pitched voice that would always elevate when he called his rottweiler, Roxy's, name. We'd have sleepovers at each other's houses and play in his wooded backyard. We'd catch crawdads and put them in clear glass jars and ride bikes off the embankments. We spent most of our time outside building things with the help of his dad. We'd ride our gas scooters with weed-wacker motors around the Old Stonehaven neighborhood, and we'd throw frisbee and explore the nearby parks, spending all day running through peoples' yards talking on our walkie talkies. We filmed home movies inspired by the MTV show, Jackass, and jump on his parents' waterbed. I knew

Hayden looked up to me, and I tried my best to set a good example. Clearly, I failed at the endeavor.

Hayden and I knew each other at a time of guilt-free bliss. Childhood was good to us, and we had been two misfit peas in an oddly shaped pod. I was the older brother he never had, and he was the younger brother I didn't know I needed. We went to the same church just up the road from his house and did our best to talk our way out of the choir. We'd go to West Virginia on mission trips and tell ghost stories as we slept on the gymnasium stage floor. We'd dare each other to say, 'Bloody Mary' three times and give our best impressions of Jar Jar Binks. We'd go to New Orleans after Hurricane Katrina to help clean up and travel to the Outer Banks on vacation.

Hayden and I did everything together, but as I got older, my big brother role fell by the wayside. I lost interest in hanging out with him. It was no longer a good look to hang out with a kid who was five years younger than me. I moved forward and went to college while Hayden stayed in Charlotte. He had only come to Boone to visit me once, and I tried to act cool by showing him how much I could drink. In less than 24 hours, he was already driving back home in fear of my behavior.

But there we all were, sitting with straggled relief under the dining room's chandelier made of delicate square pieces that, to all of us, looked like Triscuit crackers. It was the same dark wooden table I sat around growing up. The place where my grandparents sat, and Papa would say his ridiculously short but effective prayer. It was the table where my mom would set down macaroni and cheese and green bean casserole, and where I'd sprawl out notes to study for final exams during high school.

There were drinks flowing around the living room, and we all joked about life growing up. No one truly knew what I was up to and the destruction I welcomed into my life. There were no photos to bring as evidence. I deleted and reconnected my Facebook and Instagram over twenty times, erasing every photo in the process. It was my way of starting fresh. But every little effort to create a fresh start still had stains from the past. I wanted to push what happened out of existence. To freeze those experiences in the time in which they occurred. But the problems I so desperately wanted to whitewash bled over, and the photos I put in the trash can and clicked empty were still crystal clear in my head. It was a lonely feeling sitting there that night. The only way I knew how to mask how I felt was to drink.

They smiled with excitement and considered what I did, getting my degree, an accomplishment. I just got drunk that night and considered that one. To my parents, I made a huge step towards a successful life. To me, I simply got the diploma that was expected of me. The requirements of adult life were finally coming into play, and I knew student teaching would be starting in January. The reckless nature of partying all day would soon be behind me—or so I thought.

Student teaching was interesting yet revealing. I never fully enjoyed working with kids, and knew that when the bell rang and they loaded into their buses, they went back to a place unknown to me. Frankly, I didn't care; I was just glad they weren't my own. Maybe they left for a loving home or maybe not. Most kids weren't damaged yet. They smiled and drew with passion. But I knew it wouldn't last. They'd get lost in the percussion of life. It would take them where it wanted, as it did me. I knew that their innocent joy probably wouldn't last long. These were rough schools, and most kids were saying words I hadn't learned until high school. They grew up fast and without much thought.

I'd get up at 6 a.m. to drive 30 minutes south to Gastonia, the armpit of Charlotte. Driving past broken-down factories, I saw bums making their way for their morning fix. Buildings had 'Closed' signs plastered on the windows and shuttered doors. Gastonia was a place you'd only go to if you had to. Maybe it's better now, I don't know. What I do know is at the time, a lot of kids weren't set up for success.

By the time of my graduation, my parents had moved again. It was a house on Ciscayne Lane in the very neighborhood I grew up in. It had a koi pond alongside Japanese maples and a deck with wire stripes. There were pebbled paths and an old workshed where I'd smoke a bowl when I was home for the holidays.

My granddad, my father's dad, also lived there. He moved in when his beloved wife died and instantly became the breadwinner of opinions. I'd get home and see him watering the driveway. Dude did have a green thumb, but that was lost through the concrete cracks of time. I'd hear him early in the morning getting on my dad. He didn't agree with anyone, and it was strange yet satisfying seeing him treat my dad like my dad did me sometimes.

While student teaching, I'd drive to the Alpha Mill apartments and meet up with Kai, who had moved back home to attend law school. Kai was around my age, and I'd known him since we were babies. He was a wild kid with a lot of opinions and a sense of mania, much of which hadn't changed from childhood to adulthood. Kai was the kind of person who could talk his way through anything. Becoming a lawyer was the perfect fit for his personality.

As we got older, Kai and I developed eerily similar paths as we both wandered into destructive curiosity. He went to the University of South Carolina and got into experimenting with drugs. Being a smart guy, he was able to graduate in 4 years. We gradually lost contact with one another, but now that we were both back in Charlotte, it seemed that twisted fate made a fit. We made a new connection through the substances we were absorbing and were hell-bent on getting high. We did our best to royally gold plate our false prosperity. Kai's experience in law school was a first-class ticket to breaking the law. His friend Austin lived there as well. He was also in law school and finished off the trifecta.

Austin always had a Ziplock bag of molly, and I'd call him halfway home on highway 77. "Fucked-Up Fridays" became a tradition we held for at least two months straight. We'd get absolutely toasted and fry our brains with ecstasy. We stayed up all night and hung out on the roof that faced downtown. I'd drag my ass home sometime in the morning, throwing up on myself as I turned the wheel, pretending it never happened. It was tough keeping a secret, but I hid so many things from my parents already, it was just one more lie.

Student teaching was nearing its end, and my time in Mrs. Odell's classroom had been a long, dragged-out process. While I did learn quite a lot about what it took to be a teacher, I also learned that maybe the profession wasn't for me. However, I had gone too deep and knew that teaching would be the only way to make a decent paycheck moving forward. Plus, It would be expected of me to use the degree that I barely earned.

I started substitute teaching shortly after my internship was over and quickly realized how difficult finding a full-time art teaching gig might be. It was the kind of thing where most postings required two to three years' worth of experience. *How the fuck was I supposed to get a job with this requirement?* Substitute teaching was a shit job and was masked as gaining experience. However, it was an easy job. I found out high school was the easiest to teach. All I did was pass out worksheets. I didn't care if the kids did them or not. I let them go to the library whenever they wanted. That was the excuse they made to be able to roam the halls. As the summer approached, the restlessness became unbearable. It was late May and I didn't want to stick around for the hot, humid days of summer, so I started searching for jobs in Asheville. It was a town most App State graduates moved to. I knew some people there and figured it'd be a great place to spend a few months.

I browsed Craigslist for employment and eventually came across White Duck Taco, a hipster taco shop in the River Arts District. My coworkers were other twenty-somethings who lived paycheck to paycheck. We didn't get paid much and our daily tips always went to a six pack. I'd hang out with a beatnik girl named Kaylee who was also new to town. She was tattooed from head to toe. We roamed around and hung out at the house her parents bought her in West Asheville. We'd walk up to Sunnyside Cafe after a night of raging, and I'd start again just as soon as I got home.

Asheville lends itself to heavy drinking. It's a brewer's town full of restaurant and bar workers, truly the only jobs that remained in the tourist town. Kids act like they don't come from loving homes, and women grow hair under their armpits. If you don't live there, you call it unique, you call it beautiful. But behind the street art, drum circles, and 5-star restaurants is a lost group of young people trying to find their way. Many succumb to the streets and the lifestyle.

I found a place to live on Craigslist about 15 minutes from downtown. The couple who lived there smoked weed and were also restaurant workers; the guy actually worked with me at White Duck Taco. They partied hard, so we got along. I'd see them out after work; we'd pound the last of our pennies through a pint glass and wake up scrounging leftover pizza from the oven. It often tasted better the second time around. But like me, their lives were about as stable as a penguin riding a bull, and they'd often lose it after a night of binge drinking.

For instance, I would be sitting in my room working on a painting in a drunken stupor and hear shit crashing against the walls. Furniture and clothes were being tossed on the lawn, and they'd walk up and down the hallway to see who could end the conversation with one last low blow. It felt like the set of the Jerry Springer show. The police would eventually be called in by the neighbors, but even they couldn't put an end to it. I'd scrambled to hide my drugs and hoped I, too, wouldn't be dragged off to jail. These types of incidents happened at least three more times during my short stay there and strained our thin relationship which was held together by the length of our bar tabs.

The apartment complex had a pool, and I'd throw a few get-togethers there. But everyone that came dissipated like a fart in a middle school classroom. They weren't really my friends and generally took advantage of my ability to drink all day. I usually provided free alcohol because it was a habit. Without party favors, no one would come.

During this time, my brother was living in Fort Lauderdale. I applied for an Art Show in Miami with little intention to make money on my work. I threw together four paintings at the last minute, abstract paintings that held no storytelling significance.

Riley and Wyatt both came with me to witness the four-day long drug and alcohol binge. Drew provided the atmosphere we had come down for. His house had a pool and a large, mirrored table that was perfect for long lines of cocaine. It was four days of lunacy and over-indulgence. I barely hung around the art show I went down for and took my four paintings off the wall before it was even over. It was just one of many times where the chase of a good time would override the chance of a positive opportunity. Any open door I had would be closed by the worshiping of substances.

I'd get back from Miami with nothing in my pocket. I hadn't sold any paintings, and my job at the taco shop certainly wasn't a fast pass to wealth. I eventually got in over my head and couldn't afford rent. I had blown it at the bars and up my nose. A coworker asked me to get an 8ball for him. Of course, I said yes, with no intention of ever giving it to him. I took the money he gave me and took a trip back to Boone for the weekend for no fucking reason. There was no one I wouldn't screw over.

When I got back from Boone and all the money he had given me was gone, I panicked. I barely knew the dude, and it crossed my mind that people got killed over stupid shit like that. It may not have been a big deal to me, but it could have been life or death for him. Plus I fucking worked with the guy. It wasn't like I wasn't going to see him again. You can see just how well I thought all of it out. It was a way of thinking that was both privileged and entitled.

All the while Haley was in Florida working as an intern at a mental hospital. We'd talked off and on ever since we both graduated from App State, but it was nothing serious. However, as the months went on and she was reaching the end of her stint there, we planned on seeing each other. Circumstance was to play its course.

Haley would score a job as a music therapist in Chapel Hill, NC and I found my escape. I quickly packed all my shit up while my roommates weren't there. I'd still owe them rent but had no intention of paying them. I thought they'd never find me where I was going, but they'd eventually track down Haley through social media. She'd be the one that would eventually settle the debt. I was embarrassed. Embarrassed enough to screw them over. With my shit packed, I headed east towards Chapel Hill.

The drive there felt all too familiar. I once again didn't have a plan and was driving blindly. I once again screwed people over and dropped them like the bastards I thought they were. It was a five-hour drive, and I had plenty of time to think.

I pulled into Chapel Hill with my car running on empty. I didn't have enough to fill it up and would have to borrow five bucks three days later just to get to a job interview. I went to bed that night feeling like shit. I once again took advantage of people and their kindness. I was once again in a bed that wasn't mine and in a town I never thought I'd live in. Something new no longer felt like adventure.

11

Depending

I was worn out from the constant moving and bank account flops. By that point I was paying well over a thousand dollars in overdraft fees, and the one-dollar Big Mac quickly became a thirty-eight-dollar burger. I was irresponsible with money and generally woke up in survival mode. But it wasn't enough to curtail my thoughts into valuable change. It was a backwards view on what life should look like.

I was still young and in my mid-twenties. It was supposed to be like this. This was all a part of the artistic struggle. I had the laissez-faire attitude that my life would fall into place. That the constant intake of alcohol and drugs would work itself out on its own. These were the assumptions of a naive, narcissistic person. Haley would become the next person I took advantage of.

I followed Haley to a studio apartment in a sprawling complex within walking distance from downtown Carrboro. She got the apartment with the assumption that she would be living alone. It was a full circle happenstance that neither of us saw coming. She was too sweet to say no, and I moved in the few bags I had. I settled down the first night and started searching for jobs. My quick go-to was always substitute teaching because finding a full-time teaching gig was proving harder than expected. The pay was okay, and I could find work every day.

Chapel Hill was a nice town, though I tended to stay on the Carrboro side. It had an artsy crowd and was home to places like the Cat's Cradle and Orange County Social Club, a watering hole that I'd call home. OCSC was a dark bar with a colorful paper wall and a pool table. The bar had a copper surface that wound all the way from the entrance to the back where there was a jukebox. The patio was a smoker's paradise and had ivy growing up and around it. I'd end up spending or ending most of my nights there. I gave the bartenders good tips, and in return, got good service. Doing so made me feel good, but it was at my expense. Of course, the money would eventually run out.

I knew some of the regulars who were also looking for the things unseen. Being there regularly made you feel like you belonged. But it was an unhealthy place to build rapport. Why couldn't it have been a church, a volunteer organization, a sports league, or a coffee shop? Why couldn't it have been a healthy outlet? I guess for many it could be, but for me, it became a self-imploding area for destruction. That was the difference between the 'once a week' crowd and the 'every afternoon' crowd. All it took was one look at our faces.

Like Boone and Asheville, I'd give the title of 'friend' to anyone. To me, a friend was anyone who'd sit on one of those stools for hours and do several shots to cap a night. A friend was someone who had a connect, or a bag of dope back at their house. A friend was someone who wasn't there when I needed them most. It was a contradiction that fed my addiction.

I'd eventually meet a guy named Kayden and his girlfriend, Julia, who was a special education teacher. Kayden worked as a graphic designer in Raleigh and went to Savannah School of the Arts. He was a quirky guy who liked craft beer and dabbling in drug use. We all got along amongst the surface spread of liquor and beer drinks. The first night we met, I ended up on his couch smoking opium while Haley and Julia talked. Haley had her first day of work the next day, but we ended up staying up all night. She was hungover as shit and almost missed her first shift. We were both still caught up in the pattern of cooling off stress at the edge of a bar stool. Our foundation was poured with low-grade liquor and late-night hang outs, but that way of living didn't translate well to a new town.

There would soon be a dog named Benji that would enter my life. Haley and I talked about getting a dog for some time, but I didn't think we were actually going to do it. She got him from the kennel while she was back in Asheville visiting family. When someone says a dog is a man's best friend, they might just be saying that. But Benji truly was. He was my black, furry angel the size of a pint glass. Benji was a lighthearted pup, who jumped around to music and took craps at 3 a.m. I was always excited to see him after work; he would rest on my chest as I took a long nap. I brought him everywhere: restaurants, bars, and hikes. He said a lot without saying anything. He simply spoke with his big light brown eyes that seemed to capture a person's soul. He was my black velvet blanket and made me melt. Benji was able to put a temporary seal on the cracks that were slowly forming between Haley and me.

Eventually the studio apartment became too small for the three of us, so we moved across town to a two-bedroom apartment. It was a little bigger and faced a field where many nights I'd look out with a hazy gaze through the sliding glass door. By this time, I landed a full-time teaching gig in Sanford. It was about an hour drive each way. It was quite the haul, especially because I was driving my granddad's old Lincoln. It was a land yacht and comfortable as hell but terrible on gas. I drove into the sunrise every morning and listened to NPR and all the craziness going on in Syria. Hell, at least I wasn't being overrun by ISIS.

Sanford was a rundown factory town, whose prime dried out twenty-five years ago. It built an industry off brick manufacturing, which had petered off. Most of the downtown buildings had empty storefronts. Sanford's heyday was long gone. It was a depressing place; I couldn't imagine growing up there.

The elementary school I worked at was a large school placed in the middle of an open field. It had one entrance whose road made an 'S' shape towards the two-door entrance. Most teachers there were commuters and the few that actually lived in town had been there their entire lives. It was the kind of town that if you didn't leave after high school, you never would. This would be my first ever art teaching gig, and I'll admit, I was excited to start. I had faith that maybe I could make a difference in one child's heart and show them that life could be more than the empty streets of Sanford. But it was a fast realization that no change could be made by someone who couldn't change themselves. Yes, the kids were difficult and had behavior issues, but if they had the attention and patience that was needed, they could grow up to make moves in their lives. Unfortunately for them, I was a teacher whose passion faded fast. I was the type of teacher who showed up late and left early. And it wasn't long before I realized the profession I fell into wasn't going to make me happy.

The one teacher I got along with was the music teacher. She was around my age, and we would casually flirt between classes. She grew up in the area, moved away, but came home to take care of her elderly parents. She'd lock her door and vape nicotine in between classes and joke about her dating life. She was the one teacher who wasn't playing fully by the book and had a little spice to her. Nevertheless, she cared about her classes. It was that attention to her students that I never could give to mine. As soon as three o'clock hit, I was out of there and halfway down the highway ten minutes later. I didn't want to stay after hours.

I'd stop at the Harris Teeter and pick up a Jade IPA six pack. They were all gone before nightfall; it was before I turned to mainly liquor. It gave me a slow drunk; I ended up at OCSC by five. Haley sometimes came, but that eventually washed out. I was going too much and spending too much money, especially when I met a UNC grad student who sold acid. I hadn't taken acid since leaving Boone, and it was too enticing to pass up. I proceeded to trip by myself and call in sick to work.

Time was quickly going by; my weekends were never long enough. I'd ditch Haley to hang out with random people at the bar. I had met enough regulars to stay there all day. It was all about what I wanted and what I was getting.

Towards the end of my time in Carrboro, I stole money from Haley and lied to her almost every day. It was a lonely cycle of dragging Benji to the bar, so I didn't have to sit alone. He was the one friend who didn't ask anything of me. The long nights I'd spend at the bar was the only chase I had control over.

My friend Sarah who I knew from App State would move in with us in an attempt to save money on rent. I thought it was a good idea, but I'd eventually butt heads with both her and Haley. Sarah was a Phish head and followed Trey Anastasio like a God.

She was a vegan and that bothered me. Maybe it brought up bad memories of Claire from years before in Boone. She and Haley would eventually team up against me after I discarded their requests to tone down my drinking countless times.

Eventually, all things came to a familiar head, and Haley and I broke up. Just another relationship that succumbed to my behavior. Considering all of our shit was in the same apartment made it much more complicated, but I decided that going to Nashville for the summer would be a quick fix. The biggest dilemma—who got to keep Benji? I knew I wasn't going to leave without him, but before I said a word, she said I should keep him. Even though she was the one who picked him from the kennel and took him to all his necessary appointments, she still gave him to me. Something inside her knew that the four-legged furry creature would carry me out from future depths. After everything I did to her, she gave me the biggest gift of all.

I packed my shit up and left Carrboro in the rearview mirror, at least for a few months, though I'd be back at the end of summer to continue my teaching job in Sanford. I left Carrboro that summer for many reasons. Of course, there was the breakup, but there were other factors as well. For all my parents knew, I was coming to Nashville to heal from a terrible breakup, but I was running from much more than that.

In some ways, it felt like a vacation. There were no more ties to one particular person. I thought my summer trip to Nashville would be the perfect place to refresh. The next few months would be a mix of drug-filled euphoria, shame, and regretful remembrances of the past.

Nashville would become a breeding ground for bad behavior. I should've known better than to think a town built on drunk tourism could rid me of my problems. My mom and dad were happy to have me home, but my issues had yet to show their ugly head to them.

I spent that summer going to concerts in the afternoons and frequenting the bars around my parents' house. I repainted their porch and did other odd jobs around the house to make some money. I found my dad's Adderall stash and stole a shit ton. The pills lasted me the whole summer and let's just say that porch got done fast. Towards the end of summer, I'd burn out on taking them. It was getting hard to sleep and taking 2 to 3 a day had minimal effect. I gave the rest to Haley. I guess she had a slight problem too.

It was a summer where I was healing on the surface but inside, I was rotting. I stayed up for nights on end wired, making phone calls to people back in North Carolina, peeing through the open bedroom window because I was too lazy to walk the twenty feet to the bathroom, and hanging out at bars and meeting similarly disinterested people. It was three months of avoidance, and it wasn't long before I was going back to Carrboro.

When I returned to Carrboro that August, I didn't know what to think. I had moved to a new apartment and still had my Sanford teaching job. I wasn't excited about it, but Benji was in for the ride. I'd last about two months before returning to Nashville.

Shortly after school started, I'd take a deep dive into piles of cocaine and molly and was missing a lot of work. I didn't have any friends—just people that I drank and took drugs with. I tried to show a few paintings at Second Wind, a bar on the tiny town strip, but sold none. It was deflating. I questioned if I was good enough, but I had bigger problems to fry.

As the sun rose into the sky that Sunday, my brain melted with the dew that dripped on my window. My body shook and my hands trembled from the withdrawals accumulating over a month-long binger. It was at that moment I accepted for the first time that I had a drug and alcohol problem. My behavior was affecting my job, my body, and most importantly my brain. It was a realization that reality could dissolve at any minute. What started as a fun game to see who could drink the most and find the best dope became a nightmare I was fully awake for. I opened the back screen door as the humid September air hit the corners of my wrinkled eyes and let Benji out to do his business. He had no idea what was going on. To him, I had it together. To me, I hit rock bottom. I broke down, called my parents, and for the first time, admitted what I was doing. Through broken speech, I told my mom I had enough.

My parents had the 'a-ha' moment. On the other end of the receiver, they were putting together the pieces with flashes of my run-down apartment in Boone and the slow but steady distancing I did for years finally made sense.

"Stay there, dad is leaving in an hour to come get you. Everything will be okay, David. I love you," my mom said.

It wouldn't be the first time my dad would show up for me. He was a dad who saw the future for me that I couldn't.

My mom's words calmed me down, but my mind and body were in a panic. It would be the first time I really experienced a panic attack, and it freaked me the fuck out. There were so many questions running through my head. Every past move, every person I crossed, and every substance I so carelessly put into my body. I sat there alone with the shambles of destruction I had freely welcomed into my life.

I picked up the phone for one last call to Haley. She was the only person who really witnessed the daily ongoings of my life. She would come over and give me one last hug. She had tried to talk me out of my behaviors countless times before. She had tried to hold my money for me, so I wouldn't blow it on marijuana, coke, LSD, and ecstasy. She had done everything she could to set me straight. We all had problems, but mine were too big for her to handle. She looked at me with her large, yearning, dark brown eyes. It was a look of helplessness. She reassured me that I was doing the right thing, but deep down, she knew I wasn't ready to give it all up.

The last thing to do was talk to my principal at work. I couldn't just up and leave out of nowhere because the possibility of my teaching license being permanently revoked would be in the picture. I sat down in her office and was honest. Honest about the drinking and drug use, but what I of course left out was that I had been coming to work high for months. She agreed that I had to leave, and we set up a plan for me to finish out the week. I'd spend that week with my dad at my aunt and uncle's house in Raleigh, and my dad would drive me to and from work every day. He was afraid to leave me alone. I scribbled out some shitty lesson plans that would carry my absence as they searched for another teacher and packed my shit up again—this time for good—and officially moved to Nashville. My dad was in tow behind me, his truck loaded to the brim with all my things. We didn't talk about the past, but instead, my dad focused on the future. He was determined to find a solution to the problem.

Driving through the foggy mountains of North Carolina and entering Tennessee, I knew my life would change. I was leaving the state that raised me. A state with both good memories and the worst memories. It was in the very mountains that I was driving through where this all started. As they faded behind the curved road behind me, my future was once again a coin toss. It was a move I never saw coming, but it was a necessary one. Little did I know how many more twists and turns the streets of Nashville would take me.

When I crept into Nashville late that night, I had intentions of getting sober. I agreed to seek out help from a local rehab center. I called, made an appointment, and showed up at the door of an old Victorian house at the top of a hill that overlooked downtown Nashville. Would this be the place I'd finally get clean? My parents were hopeful, but as I walked through the doors, the voice in the back of my head began to whisper with immediate doubts. Why did I want to get clean? Were those nights out not some of the best times I had? At that moment, I knew I wasn't ready. I'd have to stay clean if I were to stay in the program after all.

I left the rehab center pledging to my parents that I would seek help another way. That I'd go see a therapist and attend AA meetings. But after two therapy sessions and three meetings, that plan faded just as fast as I picked up the drink again. Hell, it wasn't that bad, right? My addicted brain was good at spinning a PR nightmare into a positive take.

Not long after arriving in Nashville, I picked up Lyft driving. I knew I didn't want to substitute teach again, and it would be some time before I was able to teach art in TN. Lyft driving was a strange job. I'd pick up a wide selection of people from the wealthy neighborhood of Belle Meade to the run-down roads that branched off Jefferson Street. Like most American cities, there was a stark unspoken segregation of black and white, and it was easy to see what areas were slowly being left behind. I'd wake up before the morning rush hour and drive people to their respective destinations. Maybe to the airport, a downtown office, a body shop, or the last known place they parked their car before getting completely hammered. Everyone was seemingly going somewhere... except me. I must've driven to and from the airport a thousand times.

I'd pick up tourists who were solely in Nashville to party. A multi-day bender where people walked into the Johnny Cash Museum only to stumble into Tootsies an hour later to line dance and blow coke off the shitty bathroom sink. I only saw their faces through the rearview mirror and tried not to stare. It wasn't good money, but it was all I could find at the time. Nash Vegas, they called it. I was quickly swept up into the drinking culture.

I eventually knew every nook and cranny of the town, and I met a lot of people that had just moved there as well. They were often musicians, and I'd grow tired of hearing what instruments they played. Literally every other person was there for music. Seeing live music at every restaurant became ordinary and going to shows soon lost its appeal. I worked for almost a year as a Lyft driver and was growing tired and rusty, just like my car. The dead-end job was a silver bullet paint job I didn't want to succumb to.

I would eventually pass the Praxis exam after weeks of studying with the help of my dad's Adderall. I probably didn't need the boost but fuck it, I did nothing sober. Like literally nothing. But now that I passed the exam, I knew that finding an art teaching job would be my best shot at some decent money. And decent money meant more booze and drugs. The search would be a long and arduous process, but I eventually found a job at a middle school in Gallatin.

I didn't get the interview until mid-August, a week before school was to start. It was perfect; we were both desperate. The principal was a nice, red-headed lady, who interviewed me in a direct, informal style. When she asked why I should be hired with no experience in a middle school setting, I responded with, "How do I get experience if no one hires me?" It was a gut response, and she gave a laugh. For the first time in a long while, acting on my first thought benefited me. I'd grown accustomed to making knee jerk decisions that dropped me off worse than I was. But I think that quick-witted response that day got me the job. I had her fooled for good. Little did she know of the circumstances I left back in North Carolina.

12

Silent Shows

It was two and a half weeks until the date I was dreading; the date when I was supposed to get married. I already gave up seeking professional help and the few AA meetings that I went to never stuck. The fact was, I couldn't even complete Step 1, let alone tell the truth to anyone else. My mom would give her two cents about it all, but I'd easily shrug it off stating I knew what was best. My dad stayed distant on purpose; I think so he could be there for my mom when shit hit the fan. They couldn't afford to be equally invested. My brother and sister were equally as lost in their attempts to help me.

I spent almost every day cycling through the intense emotions of deep shame and towering vengeance. It was a mix of *what the fuck did I just do*, to *how could she do this to me?* I was actively separating myself from everyone who was capable of loving me unconditionally. I was on my own trying to figure out how I got there. I was playing the show in reverse and was trying to conjure up memories that were lost on the streets of Nashville. The past two years held a ball of emotions. But the good times were always drowned out. They were memories that flowed right into the gutter. I chose to forget a lot of things I did. But I could only run for so long. Now that Emily was gone, there was no one else to store my dirt but me.

I went to an AA meeting that Christmas Eve morning with my mom. The room was packed. It surprised me how many people were there. It was filled with people who were already locked out of their family home. The alcoholism already tore them away from everything they loved and everyone that loved them. It was depressing as shit; I fit in perfectly. I was quick to see how hard the holidays were for an alcoholic.

I sat there with my mom on the fold-out seats and listened to the stories from the strangers around me. I had been to a few meetings before but it was the first time I actually listened and wasn't high. I knew it wasn't healthy to compare, but my story all of a sudden didn't seem as bad. That's the kind of fucked-up comparisons alcoholics make in their head.

Towards the end of the hour, I got an urge to share my situation. And in a brief few sentences, I described what landed me there. Maybe it was my subconscious trying to convince me I was no different than everyone else or maybe it was a feeble attempt at self-pity. I even got a 24-hour token, a token that I would soon lose. We left the meeting, and I could see the hope for change in my mom's face. I was convinced to make a change for her, but that was the problem. It wasn't for me, and it certainly wasn't for any higher power.

As a kid, I feared God. Any slight thought about the devil scared the shit out of me. I thought he would enter my body if I thought anything negative. I thought Satan was under my bed or in my closet and would quickly close the closet door if it was left open. It's interesting where your little mind goes. I went to Vacation Bible School and church camp, learned of God's grace and mercy. But even as a kid, I was scared I would fuck it up. I was baptized of my own accord and was given a Bible and a golden cross melted from Papa's old wedding band. It wasn't long before I lost it and feared for my life.

Later that day, we went to the usual Christmas Eve Service; me, my mom and dad, brother and sister all sitting side-by-side at church. The sermon was the same as it was every year—the story of Jesus being born of a virgin to bring salvation to the human race. The people around me sang hymns with joy. Oh, they were praising God! I stayed silent while the hipster rock stars raised their hands and pranced around the stage. Those fuckers were so happy. I walked out of church with ears ringing and my mom talking about how great the service was. It probably was, but I didn't listen to a single thing the preacher said.

It was just like old times at Sardis Baptist Church when I would sleep horizontally during that terribly long hour and stare at the big circle window above the choir loft as everyone sang. I only went to church because my mom made me, and today felt no different. We all piled into the car and headed home. I knew exactly where I was going. I'd walk straight up the stairs, bobbing my head back and forth in agony. I'd stare at the wall for hours and push myself to fall asleep. The night terrors were minimizing, but they were still there. To my surprise, I still hadn't drank.

It was a familiar scene that time of year and was usually one of the few times we all got together. Like most families, it was a joyous time, but that particular Christmas, I didn't feel like being cheerful. I was still spending most of my time in the upstairs room, breaking down in tears every ten minutes. My brain was trying to heal all on its own. It was trying to patch the holes from the copious amounts of substances. It was trying to heal from the traumas I endured, self-inflicted or not.

I sat at the dinner table wondering what to say. Everyone was quiet, probably because they were lost for words. We ate to stuff our thoughts, and I was thankful we didn't have to write letters to a family member that year. My mom called it off due to circumstances. I didn't want to talk about my problems anymore. That's all I had done since moving home. My brother and dad were trying their best to keep some laughter alive. Comedy was about the only thing that could break the sticky air. I ate slowly. I ate without saying much and with a grief-stricken throat. I felt like the outcast of the family, the only fuck-up that couldn't be fixed. I felt like I traumatized everyone because, well, I had. There was no talk about Emily or the crumbled wedding.

What was Emily doing right now and what did her family think about all of this? They were fooled, just like the rest. I thought about how much money everyone lost due to the last-minute cancellations. All the food, the DJ, the tuxedos and dresses, the honeymoon, the hotel reservations… the list felt like it could go on forever and that was just the wedding tab. What the hell did I do? The series of choices I made affected people far beyond myself. People were understandably mad at me. January 19th… January 19th…

For what it was worth, I'd gotten a job at a trendy coffee shop on 12th Avenue South. It was the kind of place that sold fancy lattes and overpriced avocado toast. Although I had previous brief stints in the food industry with little satisfaction, I figured it would get me out of my thoughts for a few hours each day. At that point, all distractions were welcomed.

My parents tried their best to make the holiday feel normal, but everything felt out of place. I walked back upstairs with the guilt and shame that showered my head. I couldn't escape it. I felt grimy and the heavy feeling hadn't left. It was overwhelming, but how the hell could I get rid of it? I didn't expect it to leave for a long time.

The next day was Christmas. I was sure my sister would be up early to wake us all up. I was confident I wouldn't get any sleep. Maybe I'd hear the deer stomping on the roof above. Maybe they'd sprinkle a little Christmas cheer on my soured soul. If only I still held that childhood faith in the unknown and the unseen; the belief in a story so mystical it's hard to believe. It was hard to remember that age, but I hoped it would return to me sooner rather than later.

Christmas morning came and I laid in bed stiff as a board. As expected, I couldn't sleep. All I could think of was the daunting feat of beating what was inside me. It was like a wild beast that couldn't be tamed; like a mama bear running through camp searching for food for her hungry cubs. My parents were already up. I could hear them shuffling around downstairs. My mom, in the grace of God where she lives, was going to make that morning feel special despite the circumstances. She was probably putting the sausage casserole in the oven and taking the Kringle out of the fridge, two Newson holiday staples. They're delicious but any taste of the past had rotted. Maybe opening presents would distract me for a bit.

I remembered the year before waking up hungover, my mouth feeling full of cotton. My problems were blotted out. I changed my address several times, bouncing from place to place, deleting and blocking numbers. It was the same sick cycle, running from everything that felt uncomfortable.

I pushed myself to get out of bed. Clothes were strewn about the room, underwear with shit stains and shirts full of tears. My family was awake and waiting. Their smiles went unnoticed and my mom gave me a big hug saying, "Merry Christmas." I was glad she still loved me. I was glad I was home and not in the streets. I knew if I didn't change soon, I would be. At that point, fear might have been the only factor that drove me. The fear of disappointing family, of disappointing God. I had already crossed both, but God would be the last judge of that.

Wrapping paper was thrown across the floor, and Benji laid on top of the colorful ribbon. He had no idea what was going on or maybe he understood, but just couldn't express it. He had been through just as much as me but hadn't left my side. I loved that damn dog and wanted to give him the best. He'd been on the run with me ever since Carrboro. His big eyes were still locked on my every move. He sat calmly by my side on Christmas morning. God put that furry creature into my life for a reason. He hadn't moved an inch even when I nudged him. He wouldn't falter and wouldn't ease his closeness to me.

After temporarily masking my problems with open presents and distorted happiness, I tried to think of things to do. The Macy's Day Parade and Christmas Day basketball would soon be on the television. I was never into either, but maybe I'd give it a shot this time around. Simply sitting down to watch a simple program always bugged me. I couldn't even fucking do that. Christmas was over.

My mind was dragging me back upstairs. The place where, for so many days and nights, I sat alone. I wanted to show my parents that I was thankful for them by giving them my presence. Oh, what a gift that was. I could go for a walk, throw a ball with Benji, paint or draw. I wish I could've told myself I'd do all three, but there was little hope I would. Whatever creativity I had left was gone. It just didn't seem important anymore.

I started taking my gifts upstairs. Mostly clothes, socks, and underwear. Well, don't forget the Lifesaver book. Every Christmas my siblings and I got that sweet treat in our stockings; sweet nostalgia. The gifts were nice to get, but all I wanted was to give my parents the ultimate gift: change my life, whatever that meant. Something had to give.

2018 was coming to an end, a year that was a vicious cycle of addiction and false promises. January 1st would be just another day, but it always held significance to me, as it does for countless others. The old washes away and the new comes in. It gave me a bit of hope, but in the back of my head, I knew the show may never end. It hadn't stopped, and I'd been the puppeteer talking through false bravado. The crowd watched me flounder about, changing clothes, changing scenes, improvising through circles of regret and painful mornings. The spotlight chased me around, and it was already past intermission. It was the kind of show you shouldn't have scalped tickets for. You just overpaid and got ripped off all together.

Night fell on Christmas and I figured I'd drive around town for an hour. I needed to clear my head and think. The roads were always clear in Nashville on Christmas night. The bars would open that evening and fill with people getting a break from their families. I wouldn't stop tonight. I'd drive away from town past the mansions of Belle Meade and towards Percy Warner Park. The park where I got on my right knee and asked Emily to marry me. The road going by those formerly lush green fields would be empty that time of year. Empty enough for me to see what was in front of me.

13

Drop the Ball

Even almost two weeks into my half-assed attempt to be sober, my body still ached. I craved a drink; my brain still told me I needed it. No matter how worn out my body and mind were from years of substance abuse, I still didn't see the point of getting sober. It's absolutely crazy what addiction does to someone. I didn't think I'd ever be happy again, so I might as well be drunk and miserable. This becomes the standard way of thinking for an alcoholic.

On the morning of December 31st, I decided to get drunk. It was the last day of 2018, a day that could have represented positive change. But I decided to have one last night of partying. One last night and then I'd call it quits for good.

"Yeah, this will be it. One and done," I told myself.

I'd put it on the shelf forever after one last taste. Yeah, like that'll work, right? That night, I'd ring in the New Year the best way I knew how: watch that stupid fucking ball drop and give false hope to the future. I had nothing to lose. Had I really been happier sober the past two weeks? I didn't care what my family thought. I'd give it one last hoorah.

I had already quit my job at the local hipster coffee shop. The manager was a jerk, and I should've known better than to try and work in a restaurant again. I hated making food, prepping food, sweating over a grill, and especially dealing with chefs. They tended to be such assholes. They had me prepping food mostly, mixing ingredients into giant silver bowls and hoping I didn't fuck it up. I ghosted their ass and didn't show up for my shift. But I didn't give a damn. I had bigger things to worry about. Like how I was going to sneak in my first drink in weeks under the watchful eyes of my parents. Drew and Mattie had gone home. They were probably glad to get out of there. I could see the depressing bubble sucking their joy—the house creaked with disappointment, and I was the king of sorrow.

My windshield was iced over. My parents left to go on a walk. I finally had some time to get the bottle and get back. They wouldn't even notice I had left. It was especially cold that last day in December, although the sky was clear and the sun was out. It was the perfect day for a terrible decision. I failed to let my alcoholic brain fully heal. Two weeks was just barely enough time to start the process. I closed the biggest chance I had at getting help. The rehab was going to drug test me, and I knew right then that wasn't going to work. I was still going to drink. I was still going to smoke. What was the point of spending all of that money on a program that never had a chance of getting off the ground? It was like 2016 all over again, and I still hadn't done what I came to Nashville to do in the first place.

I turned on the car and shifted the heater onto the dash. I sat there with a rapid battle happening between what I should and shouldn't do. It wasn't like I didn't know that getting a drink might set off a train that couldn't be stopped. But the side telling me 'Don't do it,' just wasn't strong enough. In my mind, a failed engagement, the lies, and the chaos wasn't enough. Crazy, I know, but there's truly nothing reasonable about a brain hellbent on getting its fix.

There was a liquor store on West End Avenue right next to the Parthenon that I'd go to, located in an old brick building with a large Jack Daniels marquee and colorful neon signs branding the names of my favorite drinks. They would have everything I would need—a wide selection of brown and clear liquors at a decent price. My mouth watered at the thought of the colorful bottles that lined the shelves. I was done for. With the $100 my parents gave me as a Christmas gift, I would buy my poison.

My car screeched into the empty parking lot and slid into a space. There were already stacks of empty liquor boxes sitting outside. Guess the morning drinking shift arrived early. I opened the front door with a high-pitched chime and panned my eyes across the rows of bottles. It was the perfect display, like a set of fine oil paintings on opening night. I walked through the aisles on my personal art crawl and browsed the bottles based on the labels. It was how I always picked my new selections. If I had extra money, I'd always splurge on a more expensive bottle. It wasn't because I was some sort of a liquor sommelier, it was because I simply could. I guess I thought it made me look more sophisticated, like I was drinking for taste or something. I knew how they stocked the shelves: the cheaper stuff on the bottom and expensive shit on top. That day, I was somewhere in the middle and wanted something familiar. I wanted to find that taste that brought me so much comfort. It's weird how my mind was playing the days-old trick on me, blocking out all the negative emotions associated with the drink and only illuminating the careless and thought-free 'fun' parts. I wanted to find that middle ground where I didn't think about the past and didn't care about the future. That was the state of mind I wanted on that New Year's Eve.

Tonight would be the first night in a long time I wouldn't have a New Year's kiss. I'd kiss the bottle instead. Most kisses before had been glazed with liquor, kisses with an underlying meaning that masked my problems. They were kisses that put off the words that'd come in the morning, or the day after that, or the day after that. There was always a problem that would follow a night of heavy drinking, whether that was a physical ailment, a professional mishap, or a relationship blunder; a fight always followed. But tonight I wouldn't have any of those things, well, maybe besides the physical part. I didn't have a job, and I certainly didn't have a relationship to worry about. It would just be me when day would break its golden rays across the morning frost. I hadn't drunk in thirteen days, the most I'd gone for as long as I could remember. It meant I'd get drunk fast.

I walked the aisles of the liquor store for twenty minutes by that point and made a decision. My parents would be home soon and getting caught wasn't an option unless I wanted a huge fight and possible expulsion from their house. I wasn't ready to be homeless. I thought about getting vodka because I knew it was easy to mix. Vodka juice, vodka tonic, vodka by itself? Vodka really mixed well with anything. It was my go-to drink. But what else should I get? Should I make it a real one-man shit-show and get tequila? I was never a big fan, but man did it get a girl lit. However, it would just be me and the bottle in the upstairs room tonight. There was nobody to be intimate and have a night of drunken sex with. No one to touch and look in the eye as the sparklers reflected the embrace of the crowd in Times Square.

I paced the sections a while longer and landed on the gin aisle. For some reason, clear liquor was always the catch of the day. Maybe it looked lighter on the eyes, or maybe it was capable of being mixed with literally whatever was in the back of the fridge. Bombay Sapphire would be the perfect pairing to my vodka. The blue bottle glistened like a Caribbean shoreline with endless palm trees. Its alcohol content was high, which was always enticing. My mouth watered just thinking about the first sip. It was like it missed me more than I missed it. I figured I'd blow the whole one hundred dollars, fuck it.

But even with two bottles in my hand, I still wasn't done. I needed to get something else. I knew I'd get tired of the vodka and gin taste. I'd always buy a hodgepodge of drinks for that reason but in actuality, I knew I'd run out. That would be the worst. I settled on whiskey. It was perfect for a cold winter day! All I had to do was put it over ice, then eventually over nothing. My taste buds would be destroyed in no time. I made my way toward the counter and past the beer fridge. I just had to have a six-pack. With three bottles and a six-pack of beer in my basket, I finally had enough for the night. If that alone wasn't a warning sign that I had a problem, I don't know what else would be.

To my surprise, the guy behind the checkout counter recognized me. He asked where I'd been. *Had I really been there that much?* I wasn't his friend, but it strangely felt good to be recognized. It was a recognition that only fed the fuel under my alcoholic ass. I looked up at him and said I was ready for the year to end. It seemed like a common thought. If only he knew what I'd been through, he probably wouldn't have even sold the liquor to me. But there certainly was nothing he could say at the time to put it all back on the shelf. I typed in my pin with subtle remorse. I promised myself I wouldn't do it, but it was too late. Swipe-Tap-Tap-Tap-Tap-Enter. I couldn't return it now; I couldn't throw it away.

I walked to the parking lot while other patrons made their way to the entrance. They would be getting drunk tonight too, but tomorrow, they'd put it up. I couldn't. I walked across the street to the Piggly Wiggly, my car still in the liquor lot. I hoped my parents wouldn't walk by and spot it, but I assumed they walked the other way towards McCabe Greenway. I was sure I had another twenty minutes before they got home. The Piggly Wiggly smelled like a pile of wet clothes and the tile was browned like retired cold cuts. The place just smelled musty.

I made my way to the back left corner of the store and grabbed the last Limeade from the fridge. Limeade or Lemonade was always the perfect mixture for my clear drinking habits. Hell, it almost felt like a healthy summer stand drink for a quarter. It was meant to be. I grabbed the bottle and walked briskly to the checkout line. There was no telling how much longer I had till my parents got home and bringing in all this booze certainly wouldn't have been a good look. In a sick way, I got off on the thrill of being caught. It was like some sick game where I would eventually lose, no matter what.

The lady at the checkout counter looked tired. I didn't blame her. I wouldn't want to be there either, and we both looked at each other with that recognizable, 'fuck this,' expression. Maybe she, too, would be getting loaded tonight, and I cracked a 'you know I am' smile. I almost forgot the most important addition to my bag of tricks: a bag of ice. Hot drinks were the worst. Yes, they'd get me drunk, but they wouldn't be enjoyable. I wanted to at least somewhat care about what I was putting down my throat. Cold drinks just went down so smoothly. I definitely didn't want to use my parents' ice. They'd immediately know something was up, and my dad probably wanted some ice for his own beverages. I could fit all the shit into the backpack I brought.

I walked back across the street, panning West End Avenue for any familiar cars going by. It was a mix of paranoia and excitement, the thrill of the chase. Everyone whose last wish for me to get sober was soon to fly out the window. Everyone who was damaged in the wrecks I caused would be terminal. I was a one-man band playing the only song he knew— the one of an addict pursuing his last high. But I knew it wouldn't be the last.

On the short drive home with my supplies in the back, I looked in the rearview mirror with a sudden smirk. My addicted brain wasn't thinking clearly, and quick thoughts of regret would flash in and out, like a battle playing in my head. Why the hell was I doing all of this? Why the hell should I not do this? I had no clear answer. What was one night going to do? It would just be one night, right? Any mind reader would have a field day trying to keep my conscience straight. I was flailing around like a headless body. Who cared if the rest of it went?

I was back in the upstairs bedrooms, waiting for the perfect moment to crack the first one open. My parents had no idea. They were busy doing their own thing. Most people around me had already made my bed for me. They probably knew I wasn't committed to change. That I wasn't all in on giving up the bottle.

Doesn't the old saying go, "In chaos comes order"? But in that body of destruction, I'd fall, like that stupid ball in Times Square, exploding with color as it hit the ground. I'd go out in a ball of fire like a true champion of a good time. They'd say, "Didn't he live his life to the fullest? Didn't he celebrate his life justly with one last drink?" There was no cheering and there never would be. I wouldn't be alive to see it.

The clock read 3:01 a.m., and well, I was hammered. My body felt good, but my mind felt sloppy. There were open orange juice bottles sprinkled throughout the room. I didn't remember buying orange juice. And why was the window open? There were beer bottles laying on the roof. There was piss dripping from the windowpane. I didn't even remember the ball dropping. I didn't even remember which musicians performed. Not like it really mattered. It was a useless night. I had gone downstairs once just to poke my head around the corner. I didn't want them to smell the liquor on my breath. I spilled a little on my pants and shirt, and I'm sure they reeked. I guess my parents had a good New Year's celebration, but they didn't say much about it. My head hurt like hell, but regret hadn't arrived quite yet. I passed out with all of my clothes on in a rather familiar position.

It was the next morning. I didn't sleep well but the bottle knocked me out; I forgot how well it did that. There was nothing to do that day but drink again. I actually kind of wanted to start right then. The wheels were already turning. How would I sneak up a bottle or two without my parents noticing? It's interesting how my mind worked. It was already scheming for a booze-filled day of adventure. And by adventure, I meant sitting on a chair and staring at the computer screen. So how would I pull it off? I'd take a shower first. Warm water would clear my head. Oh yes, that would do it.

14

Falsifying Presence

Shit got out of hand fast. I was standing over the toilet, late at night, pissing in the dark but didn't care. I was staying up till 3 in the morning drinking every last drop from the bottle. I was driving home drunk and stopping at the corner store before stumbling home quietly through the back door. Remember, I was still trying my best to keep this under wraps. I assumed I was doing a good job but who knew, who cared? I knew my nonchalance about the situation would have its day, but the present seemed like the only thing I could grasp. It helped deal with the pain of the past. It wouldn't be long till that Saturday rolled around. That Saturday when wedding bells were supposed to be ringing.

I let myself slip back into a familiar pattern. The cycle of drinks felt like a familiar toxic friend. It had been a week since New Year's Eve, and I drank religiously every day. It was a whirlwind of nothingness and the days were distorting, my feet buckling from a blockage of alcohol. The information I gathered from the few AA meetings I went to said this would happen. They said it would call me back like a kid to the principal's office. It felt good acting out in the moment, but there would be consequences. Despite what I heard in the closed-door groups, I didn't want what they were offering. I didn't want to be some mindless sheep professing his inadequacies. I was too good for them, and their own experiences meant nothing. They said falling off the wagon the second, third, and fourth time around got exponentially worse. I'd soon find out this was horrifyingly true. For me, first-hand experience would be the only way to learn. That's the problem with most alcoholics—we are terribly stubborn.

Negativity was engulfing my world. No one knew better than me. The therapist I blew off, the pathetic circle jerk drunks, or God above, none of them could save me. It was my drunk self and all the assumptions that came with it against the world. Just thinking about the world outside my four walls pissed me off. It certainly held nothing for me by that point, so I sat there hopelessly in the upstairs attic room and watched the days pass.

I was a lousy person, a bad coworker, a terrible son and brother, and a lost soul. I pushed everyone away from me and didn't have the time of day for anything. My mom would make attempts at asking me to go on a walk, go to the store, go to dinner, watch a movie, or go to church. She repeatedly asked me to come along, but I threw it back in her face. Looking back, I can imagine how hurtful that was. She wished for any sense of normalcy in my life. She wanted me to bounce back from everything terrible. The thing was, my self-confidence was completely shot and I lashed out on anyone I could.

I'd look out the familiar small window like many times before and see people walking by living their lives like normal people. Life was in many ways a game. A game I was losing. How bad was it to go to a job, make money, and live an honest life? How bad was it to open up about my struggles to strangers in a room and see a therapist to heal from my past? To a clear-thinking mind, absolutely nothing. But to a brain buttered up on high-grade liquor, it was practically impossible.

It was a sinister view on life that only grew with every drop. Knowing that people sucked up to people they hated. To bosses that would never give them a promotion. Going to church to mask their sins. But, nevertheless, waking up every day with a positive outlook on life. For me, life was a dim and boring event that meant nothing. I had no purpose in society, and society had no place for me. I was only out for myself, and people would have to meet me where I was. I was the judge of my one-man court and to me, everyone was guilty. It didn't matter who you were. You crossed me and did me wrong. There was no person I wouldn't write off, and that included everyone in my family.

My mom would push books about drug addicts and alcoholics who got clean by a miraculous act of God, but I'd nitpick all their other shortcomings. They hadn't really changed, and they certainly weren't any better off than they were before. It was like no good story was actually true. My pessimism was taking complete control of my life. Not one person could give me a good enough reason to stop drinking. Even when I lost so much, I couldn't see the point. As strange as it sounds, it was the only sense of normalcy I could find. And it was that normalcy that was tearing me into something unrecognizable.

If I wasn't up in the attic, I was at the bar. I'd sit with the regulars and spend my last dime on booze, forgetting dinner. I was revisiting places that stole everything from me. Tipping big to the bartenders that "missed" me, staying up until 2 a.m., hitting on women who seemed interested. They thought I had my shit together, but my car was running empty. They thought I was going places, but I was only thinking about the bar down the street. They thought I had my own place, but I was living at home. I told lies they'd never find out about. I had my glass-bottled friend right in front of me. It didn't nag me. It didn't have a personality to deal with and friends to falsely like. It didn't have wants and needs. It didn't take my kindness for granted. It kept me warm and safe.

It was a few days away from *the* day, the day I was supposed to be getting married. I stuffed Emily on the back ring and burned her well. I did my best to forget about what I did to her. I would rather close that book without forgiveness. I said I was sorry, but it didn't mean much. It was too traumatic of an event to forgive. No one on her side of the family would ever reach out to me again. They were done.

I was better off alone. I was better off not consoling people who had a bad day, waving to people at crossing walks who never wave back, handing out change to people at red lights. I didn't give a shit about anyone's situation. People had taken from me for too long, and now I was giving myself what I needed. I was riding around town with my copilot in the black bag.

I told myself my body felt fine. I told myself my mind was intact. I told myself everything would work itself out if I just kept riding. It was the kind of thinking that barely got me out of the previous ditches. The kind of thinking with a mix of 'hell yeah' and 'holy shit.'

I was a mix of deep sadness and smoldering anger. I told myself she did me a fucking favor. The chains were broken. No more ragtag ball of emotions or guilt for coming home late.

All I needed was the cold cured drink that flowed down my throat and struck my heart with adrenaline. I didn't need anything but that. Well, I needed a job, but I wasn't paying rent at the moment. I could probably milk it a little bit longer. At least long enough to find a decent job and move out.

The ridiculous dreams and night terrors full of emotion would whittle away with every sip. No more thinking about how to resolve the mess I made. Through drunk eyes, it looked a little pretty...like an abstract painting I could sell for thousands. There was a purpose to a wreck. There was a point to my subliminal actions. I assumed there was value in the pain I caused. Telling myself a lie simply felt better.

2019 could be something great. I could ride this bike alone. Ride it into the horizon and watch the glare from the motorcycle blind the fools behind me.

Emily could live her own life. That's what she wanted, right? Well, here you go. Instead of trying to change me into a yoga loving yes-man, she could determine her own life goals. She could marry someone else and alter that fuck's dreams.

I wasn't going to listen. I wasn't going to change. I had everything I needed. Good riddance to guilt. Good riddance to shame. I had it in my hand. My addictions were just getting reheated.

15

Emily

It was only a few days from the called-off wedding and no matter how much I tried to drink myself away from her, I could still see her face. Even though I drove to different areas of town, I was still tuned to familiar sites. Even the bottle couldn't blur the many nights we fought leading up to the split. I thought about packing up and running off to somewhere else, maybe North Carolina, but what would that do? I learned that no matter how many times I changed scenes, it was still the same play.

I first met Emily on 12 Avenue South in 2016. She was with her happy-go-lucky friend, Scarlett. Understandably, she didn't want to meet a complete stranger at the bar alone. I went on the dating app, Bumble, with unsure intentions a few weeks after moving to Nashville. I figured it would be a good way to get laid and move on from Haley. I stumbled upon Emily by chance after laying my thumb on 'right swipe autopilot.' I was too lazy to go through all of the bios and figured I could filter out the 'good' ones after the fact. I was single for just a few months and was already looking for companionship. It was a cycle that I couldn't break.

I was sitting at the bar when they walked in. I breathed a sigh of relief when I saw it was the same girl from the pictures. She was a small, skinny girl with a big smile and wavy highlighted brown hair. She had on tight blue jeans, small heeled brown boots, and a black blouse. She sat down with a wholesome grin across her face and talked with a small country accent. I guess she was happy that I, too, was the guy in the photos online.

She looked at my beer and asked what it was. Little did she know I moved to Nashville to get sober. What she didn't know couldn't hurt her, right? I had gotten used to creating relationships with a pint glass in hand, and it was the only way I knew how to slide in. Emily was also from North Carolina and ironically went to UNC, the place I had just fled, for her undergraduate. She had lived on the Chapel Hill side while I was on the Carrboro side. They were two sides that many tended not to cross.

Emily moved to Nashville to attend graduate school at Vanderbilt. Clearly she was smart, but not smart enough to see through my problems. I was good at masking them by that point, playing the game of trickster for as long as possible. We talked for two hours and agreed to meet up the next day at Percy Warner Park.

The next day, I was sitting on a grassy bank with Benji, waiting for her. She was thirty minutes late but was cute enough to call to tell me she wasn't ghosting me. She stepped out of her car in jean overalls followed by her dog Ruby. Ruby was a lunatic and bounced around like a cat pouncing for the laser pointer. She and Benji would eventually get along. We started walking up the concrete path that wound through the woods. It was the beginning of fall, and the trees were starting to change colors. The cool air gave me goosebumps, and I was somewhat nervous about how smoothly the conversation would go without any alcohol to loosen my tongue. Luckily, we were clicking, and I couldn't help but suggest we go to Yazoo Brewing. There wasn't even a slight chance I would go an entire day without a drink.

We stopped by the brewery for an hour and eventually ended up at her house. It definitely wasn't going to be mine, considering I lived with my parents. I was surprised she already extended an invitation there and wasn't turned off to the fact that I was a twenty-six year old living at home. It was embarrassing, but she knew I was there because I was trying to get back on my feet. That wasn't a complete lie.

We got to her house, and I brought in the backpack full of liquor I stored in my trunk. I didn't want my parents to find it while I was out that day. She laughed at the fact that I had a 'party bag' ready to go. Looking back, that should've been the first big red flag. She stopped drinking while I continued to pour myself one, and we talked for a few more hours before closing the evening with a kiss. It was a kiss that kicked off a relationship that would almost go all the way.

Emily was a smart girl who studied poverty and its effects on disenfranchised populations, an ironic topic for a privileged white girl. She was driven to help people and had a natural tack for caring. She was a teacher who probably cared too much. I always viewed my teaching job as a 'show up, then leave' situation while she stayed after school and even drove some of her students home. It felt like she was overly involved, but maybe that was because I was too inwardly flawed.

Her house was on 12 Avenue South, just past the park and over 440 on the left. It was two stories high, and she lived with a roommate who was also a teacher. The roommate was from Alabama and taught math, two things I struggled to understand. Her roommate had a cackle laugh that would drive anyone nuts and food prepped on Sunday evenings, completely wrecking the small kitchen. I pretended to be her friend while I stole her jar of Oxycontin and weed from her terribly hidden stash after a quick peruse around her room. Doing so put me on edge for several months as I waited for the hammer to drop, but it never did. It was the kind of exhilaration that any drug addict could get off on. I got away with it, which in my sick mind made it okay. Emily would never find out, along with countless other low-life escapades.

Emily and I would end up creating a lot of memories in that brick house, some good and some bad. We would sit on the porch while the dogs played in the yard below and make dinner together in her tiny kitchen. She wasn't the best cook but was good at making quiche. We'd watch movies on her couch and pig out on pizza, her favorite food. We'd come home from a late night out, taking our clothes off with every step we took up the stairs. It was the kind of budding romance that would sweep anyone off their feet... the kind of romance that was probably too good to be true.

We'd sit up in her room on snow days and people watch out of her window. The seasons would change, and we weren't close behind. We'd take walks down her street and pick which houses we liked the most, criticizing million-dollar homes that we could never afford. As the months turned to years, the brick house became too small, and just like so many things in Nashville, it was time for change. We had walked up and down 12 Avenue South enough times and the "I Believe in Nashville" mural became a haunting paradigm.

Emily was growing tired of teaching at a charter school and several buckets of tears later, she decided to quit and get a new job at an over-funded nonprofit that seemingly helped the neighborhood in which it resided.

Emily moved into a tan bullet house in East Nashville. It was a part of town that was fairly new to me, more run down than West End Avenue and 12 Avenue South. It was the 'artsy' side of town, an odd term I kept at arm's length ever since leaving the School of the Arts. A year after meeting her, I was still living at home. It was hard to save money while driving for Lyft and spending every dime I had on booze or cheap dates. I did the bare minimum to string her along.

I slowly moved in with Emily after her move to East Nashville. It was a move that would define the next 4 years of my life and isolate me from my family just over the Cumberland River.

It started out sweet with high hopes, but blackness and valley shadows were soon captured in grief. My drinking started slowly, maybe two or three beers at the end of the day, but it doubled—then tripled—fast. I couldn't hide my true behavior for long. She eventually saw how out of control I really was.

No amount of pleading or prayers could stop it. Emily became an afterthought. I'd ditch her to drive up to Lipstick Lounge. Although it was considered a lesbian bar, it catered to all types of people. I was looking to get fucked up and the bartender Victoria gladly over-poured my drinks with straight liquor. It wasn't long before I came across a guy named Owen who seemed to always have cocaine and Adderall on him. We'd hang out while Emily was sitting at home. She always had a bad feeling about him; she wasn't wrong. Of course, I refused to listen.

When you're an alcoholic and drug addict, living with someone becomes a hassle. You wake up as early as you can just to get by with shit, or at least I did. And creative or not, I always found something to do before 9 a.m. Smoking, drinking, throwing out the empty bottles I hid in the closet the day before; these things would have to get done before she woke up. Otherwise, there'd be hell to pay. Being the avoidant fuck I was, I did my best to cover my tracks. Who was I kidding? She wasn't an idiot.

When she got up, I'd hug and give her a kiss like everything was okay, and she would venture off into the bathroom. I'm sure she knew what I was doing but most days, she didn't say anything. It wouldn't be until the last months when she'd finally confront everything. Every time she didn't say anything, it was just another positive reinforcement that I could get away with things. It wasn't her fault. It was a fucked up game I was determined to win.

We were growing apart for months and at that point, the lies were constant. I was usually at the bar but didn't want her to know. We'd argued about what to do on Saturday morning. I just hoped she wouldn't join. She grew tired of my jokes and weary of the repeated attempts at happiness. Honestly, I didn't know how to be happy. And I continued to search for happiness through Owen and other people at Lipstick Lounge. It was the one place I could escape to that normalized how I felt and what I was doing.

Sometimes, I'd also go to Vinyl Tap, a new spot I discovered at the edge of Inglewood and Five Points. It was a trendy place that poured decent drinks and sold vinyl music. It was a place that complemented Lipstick Lounge well and was just down the road. If I wasn't at one, I was at the other. On a good day, I'd drag Emily to Vinyl Tap for a drink. She refused to go to Lipstick Lounge after she met Owen and a few other loathsome others in the group.

I didn't know what to think anymore. I made a series of eight paintings of things I thought would be important. They were paintings of everyday scenes around the neighborhood. Images I conjured up in a drunken mind. Pictures of discarded red chairs in the alley, the Ferris wheel at the state fair, Benji sitting below the trees at Shelby Park. They sat, still and colorful. But the person that made them was living in black and white. They ended up flopping on the slanted wooden floor and getting ripped with a knife. Don't call me irrational, but also don't doubt my thoughts, which I thought were well spread on gesso.

I made continued promises of seeking help, getting sober, and not lying. All those promises were lost in a matter of days, sometimes hours. I'd get sober for a week or two, then fall even harder when I reentered the devil's cage. Emily and I would road trip to Montana and back, go to different restaurants or state parks, and attempt to make friends in small groups at a new church we'd attend. But all these things were done half-assed. I was too preoccupied with myself to think about any other person, including her. These failed promises would become the catalyst for departure.

A relationship that was held up on thin stilts eventually fell. It was a relationship that was built on lies and false promises. It was a relationship that left both parties flat on their faces.

There were no winners in this game I started, only broken hearts and hopeful goodbyes. No matter how much attention, how much love, or how much support she gave me, she couldn't get me sober. It was just another tragic example that change would have to come from me and me alone.

16

The High of Love

We went to the food tasting for the wedding. I saw the upstairs room where I'd put on the tux and get those cliche behind-the-back shots of me tying my bow with the wedding party standing beside me. I saw the place where we'd take our newlywed photos and the road where we'd take the car out that had a "Just Married" sign on the back. I saw the grand table where a feast would lay, the altar where I'd say, "I do." I saw the big oak trees where I'd see my future branching in front of me. I saw all these things high as a kite on pills.

I ate the food high on Adderall and pushed away a lot of it. It was farm to table, coming straight from the garden on the property. Emily asked me what I liked, and I just agreed with a nod. I put the burden all on her when she had already done so much. There she was, sitting next to me with a joyous smile of excitement. Her childhood dreams of wearing the white dress and having an extravagant wedding were coming true. She had anticipation in her eyes. I couldn't look at her. My heart was going a mile a minute. Our wedding planner eventually showed up, someone I never saw or talked to before. Another example showing how uninvolved I was. I took the "whatever you want" approach and said yes to everything. I was disassociated with everything to do with the wedding. I cared enough to share in the novelty of getting married but not the commitment of marriage. She had a ring that I bought to make myself feel better. I'm sure she noticed that I was distant, but she pushed forward anyway. She loved me and I loved her— but I loved other things more.

We went to marriage counseling a few times before our wedding date. The sessions were pretty intense, and she broke down several times after talking about the past year we had. I'd be lying if it didn't break my heart into shreds. In our last counseling session, I hit a giant brick wall. Our original counselor was out on maternity leave, and her husband stepped in to fill the gap. I wish he wouldn't have.

He struck me to the root of my core when he asked if quitting drinking meant I could keep her. I thought, *Who is this asshole? Who is he to tell me what I should do?* He was playing directly into her hands. And now he expected me to bow down to him, too. I had no plans on doing that. I touched the edge of her knee in an effort to try and comfort her, but I chose the sauce. *Did that fucker not want us to get married?* I literally just met him. I stormed out of the room in complete anger and disbelief over what just happened. I was never going back to him again. Emily reluctantly agreed to not see him anymore.

Everything was planned and ready to go. Guests had hotel reservations, flights, and their best attire ready. It's embarrassing to think of all the plans I ruined, all the people I tricked into sending us gifts. People were excited to celebrate us and to send us off into the oblivion of marriage.

It all came to a head the week after we got back from visiting her brother in Fort Worth, Texas. Her brother had just adopted a baby and she wanted to go see him. I reluctantly went along, knowing I'd be miserable the entire time. My routine would be knocked off, and I wouldn't be able to wake up at the crack of dawn to drink and get high. I almost didn't go but knew that would just cause a fight.

I got plastered the last day we were there. I'm talking black out drunk around the whole crew, including the baby. I didn't care if the infant saw what I was doing or if it was scared of me. I didn't care what kind of example I was setting. And I certainly didn't care what her brother and his wife thought. Her brother was a preacher at the local church and I'm sure he had his own opinions about me, after the countless times of watching me drink myself into a coma. I could bet that I certainly wasn't someone he wanted his sister to marry.

Emily and I fought on the way home from the trip and arrived back in Nashville that Sunday on the verge of breaking up. She demanded I get help and see a professional. I reluctantly agreed. I set up an appointment for the next day, knowing I wasn't going to show up. Of course, she'd find out, but by that point, I had two feet out the door and a bar tab already open.

That Monday night, I went out in a blackened haze following a huge fight about me not showing up for therapy. I went to Lipstick Lounge to meet up with Owen, do cocaine, and whatever other stimulant he had in his pocket. It was the last straw for her. The relationship was done. She couldn't take one more lie. She couldn't take one more promise that was broken. Love had been scattered in the dead flower garden on the side of the house. It was beyond watering.

Emily would fly out that Tuesday afternoon to escape the monster I became while I proceeded to go on a bender for several days. I couldn't tell you where I went or what I did. There was no point in reaching out to her because she made her decision. The wedding was off.

I'd pick Emily up from the airport the following weekend in a last ditch effort to save the relationship and continue our path to marriage, but we both knew that wasn't going to happen.

The mailbox would continue to receive save the date confirmation letters, a sad reassurance of what was. People sent us presents from our wedding registry, nice things that were scattered throughout the apartment and ready to use. But all that shit went to waste. Wasted like the state I was in. I left almost all of it with her, along with the ring. There was no way in hell I could take it back, and I'm sure she sold most of it on eBay. I'd later see her veil on Facebook marketplace. Maybe she made up all the money she and her family lost.

I only saw Emily one more time after what would have been our wedding day. It felt like two strangers meeting. We'd meet at the old dog park at the edge of Shelby Bottom where we'd bring Sabi and Benji to. I guess she wanted to see if I really started to make changes in my life, but it was very clear to her that I had not. The love was gone. There was too much hurt to care about each other. It was impossible to repair. It was like every memory was condensed into the last thing we said to each other. The good times were too far and too few in between. She deserved better, and I needed to get help. Unfortunately, breaking down my ego and seeking that help was no closer to me than Emily once was. My life was a mess, and it was my fault. Emily was no longer a target. Her heart had been pierced too many times to count.

I continued to think about her once everything crumbled, but I did nothing to better myself or amend what I did. Frankly, I didn't think I could ever fix everything I messed up. It was just too big to address. I was lonely, lonely like everyone else I saw at the bar. I was going out just to get away from my parents' house and escape my problems.

"You're weak."

"You're stupid."

"Your problems aren't that bad."

The hamster wheel turned faster. My body felt frail and my mind was bruised. January 19th was a day away. The day I was dreading. I didn't know how I'd feel that morning, but time would continue with or without me.

It was cold and rainy the morning of the wedding. The droplets fell from the gray sky gradually turning to soft snow that fell left to right, twirling like a dancer performing their last act. The ground wasn't cold enough, so it melted instantly on contact. I knew it was supposed to rain that day, but I didn't know it was going to snow. I couldn't seem to escape that shit. It was like Boone continued its hunt on me. I guess God had other plans.

My body felt cold and my cracked lips had nothing to say. My friend Riley was driving over from Charlotte to offer me some support. She was coming to help me get through every minute. She was supposed to be in the wedding, but now she'd share in the darkness that would eventually fall that day. She could share in my misery.

It's a weird position to be in when the biggest event of your life is canceled—and it's all because of you. The one event that was going to change your life was no longer happening. It's strange to think about everything you imagined disappearing like a good dream. I'm sure it was even worse for Emily. The tux I was going to wear gathered dust in the closet, and all my plans for that romantic night were stuffed in the sock drawer. It feels strange when you expect two hundred people to show up and only one does. I was glad Riley was coming. She was the only one who offered to come.

I grabbed the bottle from under the bed and poured myself a drink with some orange juice. It was only 8 a.m., but fuck it. I wanted to wash the pain down the drain with the melting snow, but the precipitation just kept coming.

We bounced around from bar to bar all day. I was just trying to hold out until I passed out. We tried to avoid the present and although we giggled a lot, there was no way of avoiding how I felt. We talked about college days and the misadventures we had on a weekly basis. They were funny, but they landed me in that bar seat. I was buckled in on a ride that wouldn't stop.

It was late in the afternoon, and the snow was falling steadily. It reminded me of those late nights I'd spend in Boone looking at the sky and wondering how I was going to move forward and accomplish my goals, most of which were based on the idea of just getting through another day. I was still unable to think too far in the future. By 5 p.m., Riley and I were sauced. We hadn't eaten much all day. I figured it would only take away from the buzz.

As 7 o'clock arrived, nearby church bells clanged around the corner. I didn't expect to hear them. Maybe it was just in my head. *Dong, dong.* My stomach dropped, and my arms and legs grew weak. My vision tunneled and the cold January air numbed me beyond repair. I paused to let the moment hit me, and the tears flowed out like lava flows from hell. My self-defiant ego burst into smithereens. It tore down the armor I put on and stabbed me in the heart. I completely lost it and crumbled into myself. The time to face reality clanged again as 7:01 approached. I put my drink down and looked at Riley saying, "I can't do this." She reminded me that I was strong. I knew I was a coward. I was scared like a little boy who lost his mother.

What was Emily doing right now? Was she thinking about me? Did she feel alone too? I couldn't help but wonder. The sky closed around me and swallowed me whole. I didn't look up, I looked down. I didn't dance in resistance, I deflated like a popped balloon. Every drink I guzzled to forget failed. Every person that said it would be alright, I didn't believe.

Riley comforted me the best way she knew how. Without her, it would have been significantly worse. I was glad she was there. It said a lot about her character. We continued to bounce around town in and out of bars. I was toast and I knew tomorrow would be even harder. The day after that would be, too. The promise I made to myself three and a half weeks ago to stop drinking failed, and the ball started rolling ever since the new year began. There was no stopping it now. I was by myself again. Just me, my thoughts, and my bottle.

17

The One

My drinking momentum quickened, and I couldn't stop it. Worst of all, I was hiding it. Alcohol was hidden everywhere—slid under the mattress, tucked into the top of the closet, stationed behind the toilet seat, layered under piles of clothes, clanking in the trunk of my car. Mini bottles were the easiest to hide—I hid them in coat pockets, socks, shoes, and unkempt laundry. The hardest part was finding a place to throw out the empties, the evidence. I usually put them in old grocery bags and packed them in with the normal trash. I could at least bring it down when my parents were home.

Surprisingly, I landed a job teaching watercolor painting at Vanderbilt's Sarratt Art Studios. I was surprised I got the job, and I think it surprised everyone else too. It seemed prestigious and it looked good on paper, but I simply was unable to care. It was just another teaching job, like all the other ones that came before. Another job that felt empty. Another job where I promised to do my best but did the minimum.

The Vanderbilt kids felt way smarter than me; they looked down on me. They'd ask where I went to school, expecting a prestigious master's degree. When I told them, they'd smirk with surprise. It was unsettling to be looked down upon by people who were so much younger.

My insecurity paired with my drinking made me the worst hire Vanderbilt made in awhile. I brought drinks to the classroom, and I'm sure they smelled it on my breath. I hadn't been caught yet, so I continued the trend. My boss would pop his head in the room, and I'd manage to not slur a few words. I only taught three classes, but it felt like twenty. The minutes would drag on for those three long hours, and as weeks went by, the students thinned out, dwindling down to two or three that showed up ten minutes late. Eventually, no one showed up at all.

I'd get there at 1:59, a minute before class was to start and sit in the dark room. I'd sit there, hoping no one would show up so I could leave early. I didn't want to be there, but I needed the paycheck. How else would I pay for my next bar tab? I'd sit there drunk with a cup of mixed liquor in a coffee cup and put my head down on the table wondering how I'd get through the remainder of the week. I knew why the crowd thinned out. *Who would want to be taught by some slimy, drunk twenty-something?* The class became a time where I retreated at the end of a long set of tables and drew scribbles across the pad of paper I stole from the art cabinet. If a student asked me a question, I'd answer reluctantly. The class became a soul-sucking venture that no one wanted to attend. What was more disappointing was that everyone had paid for the class. It surely was a waste of money, but I didn't care. I was still getting paid. I was a brick on a wall, and not the most welcoming one.

Although I taught for many years, the act of teaching art never really caught my attention. I grew up in a home where my mother made teaching look so rewarding. She taught with such passion and attention to her students. She made it look easy, but I quickly realized how hard it really was. My mom would have students who moved onto high school but still visited her classroom. She had students who'd give her tons of gifts during Christmas and even a large drawing of our old dog, Sandy. It was clear to me how much her students adored her. The most I got was a handful of Hershey kisses and a $5 gift card to Starbucks. I didn't like either.

I didn't know how to break art-making down into small bits so students understood. I couldn't remember how I learned to make art. I couldn't remember what about it first interested me. Maybe it was a quiet place I could retreat to as a young kid. Or maybe it was an activity that wasn't sports, or basketball, and made me feel unique. Or maybe it was because I had a natural eye for it. At that point, sitting in a Vanderbilt classroom, I couldn't put a finger on why I was even there. Drawing or painting didn't feel important, and the purpose of it all left me. Teaching was a way to say I used my degree. I thought it would be a good way to make my parents feel better about spending all that money on college. But it was a path that didn't pair well with drinking and doing drugs. *What kind of job would allow me to drink or smoke all day? Now that would be the life*, I thought.

Believe it or not, while miserably showing up to Vanderbilt, I was also dragging myself to work at another school. I was also teaching elementary art at a charter school in East Nashville, and I hated it to the core. It was a place where the past stuck to me. It was the school Emily worked at when I met her. I got the job a month before our relationship fell apart and didn't have another option. I assumed everyone who worked there already knew what happened, so my guard was up from day one.

The work environment that Emily always complained about was still the same. I already knew all the teachers' names and the dirt that came along with them. I wasn't there to start shit and avoided all unnecessary contact with my coworkers, but avoiding Emily became impossible. She started her work at the nonprofit, which was associated with the charter school. My kindergarten classes were at the center, so I ran into her every few days. Can you say awkward?

Breakups are strange. We'd pass each other like we never met. You hold all these memories of the person inside of you. Pass by places you once went. Remember things that happened on certain streets. You can't seem to escape it, but you can't seem to start anew. It's strange to think that you will never see that person again. They go on with their lives, date new people, move far away, and grow old, far from where you will eventually rest.

I planned on spending the rest of my life with her. Now I wasn't even spending a single day with her. It felt like my past was behind every corner and every door. My work circumstances made it hard to move on. I looked at her face and recognized it, but it had changed. Every day meant one more change in the way I looked at her. I'd ride up to the job on my motorcycle in an attempt to look hard and appear like I forgot. But between those five gears was angst that struggled to be released with every shift.

A teaching coach was working with me, but most of his ideas seemed bogus. He'd jump in front of the classroom in an effort to model management techniques, but the kids gave him hell. Like usual, they were out of control. He'd later get fired.

It felt like the kids ran the school. The administration was terrified of losing parents, especially those who donated money so they could write it off on their tax return. They prided themselves on innovative programs and an inclusive learning environment, but if there was no discipline, what was the point?

Going to work drunk became the new normal. I'd wake up in the morning and mix my lemonade with two or three mini bottles. I'd get back from the day's work filled with regret... but not enough to stop. But going to work drunk eventually had its repercussions. One day, I completely lost my shit and exploded in anger. The students had made a complete wreck of the paint I gave them and weren't listening to a single word I said. The room matched the way my foggy mind was thinking. I proceeded to rip up every single bit of artwork the kids made that day. Looking back, this was probably a horrifying experience for them. The consequences were harsh, and the hammer came down hard. The parents found out and slowly urged the principal to push me out.

The principal eventually pulled me aside and told me I didn't fit the school atmosphere. She wasn't wrong, but at the time I thought it was blasphemy. It was as if, all of a sudden, I cared about what I did. I walked off the job twenty minutes later. I thought to myself, *Fuck her and fuck that school*. My ego was flying high. I was heated. I didn't need that job. Once again, teaching didn't pan out, but I had a whole afternoon to kill. It wasn't hard finding something to do.

I had been off the dating market for two months, and I told myself I'd give it a year. But with my impulse control lacking, I jumped back onto dating apps and scrolled to find my next unknowing victim. I wasn't healed from the pain of losing Emily, but the loneliness I felt was getting harder. I was too uncomfortable spending time with myself and continued to drown myself with female distraction. I didn't want the failed marriage to define me. I could meet anyone and tell any story. I didn't have to be the person who wrecked an engagement. I could be the person who had accomplished whatever he said.

I eventually met someone on the East side of town. Her name was Eliana. She was an intelligent woman who was a few years older than me and worked for a publishing company. Eliana had a librarian look, with short brown hair and glasses, and she was sexually promiscuous. She had recently divorced and was just looking to have fun. There were no strings attached; it fit my situation perfectly.

She owned a small two-bedroom house on Gallatin Road. She hated going there and was persistent on feeding her refined taste. I acted like I had the money to treat her to everything while my bank account struggled to hang above zero. It was a friends with benefits situation, but for some reason, I offered to pay for everything I could. It was a situation that had a time stamp. She had two dogs and liked riding on the back of my motorcycle. She was the first woman to have enough grit to get on. We'd hang out a few days a week and even go camping one weekend.

When I wasn't hanging out with Eliana, I'd be with another girl named Aria. I had to have a backup plan in case Eliana disappeared. Aria was an innocent girl who lived in Germantown, and I made little effort to learn much about her. I was jaded on women and didn't care if what I was doing was wrong.

It felt weird bouncing back and forth between the two, but it was a nice distraction from all the problems I was running from. My connections with Eliana and Aria were surface level at best, and I was okay with keeping it that way. I was tight about opening up about the realities of my past. They didn't want to hear it, and I didn't want to share it. As long as I kept the appearance of stability, they didn't ask any questions. And as long as I picked up the tab at the end of the night, I was getting lucky. But it became clear that my wallet wasn't fat enough.

My ego was growing bigger by my natural ability to play women and get what I wanted from them. And the sad part was I felt good about it. I was filling a side of me that was lost to monogamy. I was a gigolo wearing his biggest condoms.

18

Seeking Without Substance

My parents became sick of me living at home after many fights erupted over the general disengagement I embodied. It was like a stranger was living in their home. If I wasn't out, I holed up in the attic room. I'd come home and dart directly to the stairs giving a short hello and avoid any conversation regarding my state of mind. My mom was aging faster than time expected. She slowly developed dark bags under her eyes from a lack of sleep and the wrinkles on her forehead got deeper with every development of stress. She was a mom stuck. She knew what was best for me, but her words meant nothing. My coffin was already sealed. She knew she would lose a son if nothing changed.

In spring of 2019, I moved into an apartment in Bellevue. It didn't seem like the best situation, but I was willing to do anything by that point—I had to get out of my parents' house. It was a place I hoped would work out; however, my past experience with roommates was terrible so my expectations were low.

I pulled into the complex past the small lake and walked upstairs to the apartment on the hill. It was a dark apartment with one piece of furniture—a couch that was gathering dust in the living room and trash bags filled with empty microwave meal containers. The one thing that was completely stocked was coffee because the guy who lived there worked at Starbucks.

I walked down the long hallway and past my new roommate's room where a mattress laid on the floor, clothes strewn throughout. My room was the corner room that had been left empty for some time. There was an odd depression throughout the space, and you could almost feel the arguments that previously took place there.

My new roommate seemed nice and offered to help me move my crap. He quickly told me he didn't drink and was attending AA meetings. God was trying to tell me something, but I didn't see it then. At that point, I wasn't about to stop. I didn't want to be a dick, so I kept my booze in my room. It would be more convenient to access there anyways.

The apartment was quiet. My roommate worked a lot of hours and used Uber to get there every day. I never offered to give him a ride. There was also a girl who occupied the third room. She decorated her space with fantasy statues and Gothic paintings. It wasn't my style, but whatever floats your boat. She was standoffish and her boyfriend was even worse. He didn't like me for the sole reason of me being a guy. I guess he thought I'd hit on his girlfriend. Yeah, she wasn't my type.

My roommates kept the lights off to save money. It was a musty place and smelled like an ashtray. I have a strong belief that dogs have a good sense of positive and negative energy, and Benji seemed off there. He kept his head down and stared blankly out the window. He stopped barking at the birds and squirrels going by. The dog in him seemed drained.

I was still seeing Eliana, but the spark was fading. It didn't feel right anymore; not to mention I was surprised I hadn't caught some sort of STD. I was probably her Tuesday call boy. Whatever the case was, it was starting to gross me out, even for my standards. She only came to my place once and gawked at it. To her, I was still a kid stuck in his college ways. She wasn't wrong, but if I was immature, why was she still seeing me? Her opinion meant very little to me.

I didn't talk to my parents anymore. They felt far away, although they only lived five miles down the road. I didn't want them to know what I was doing; I wanted my own life. I didn't want to hurt them with my drinking. It seemed like the lies, the avoidance, and the denial was killing them slowly. I couldn't look them in the eyes anymore with any sort of integrity.

My situation at the new apartment went downhill fast. I had just got back from my brother's wedding in Charlotte where I managed not to drink. Everyone knew I had a problem, and I didn't want them talking behind my back any more than they already were. Everyone said I was strong for being there, like I should get some sort of trophy for showing up to my only brother's wedding. Yes, it was hard and deep down I resented him for being so lucky. But he didn't have the problems I was carrying. He had seemingly moved on from his crazy days unscathed. I rushed home as fast as possible knowing I'd see Eliana that night and get laid. At least that would stop the bleeding wound for a bit.

Not long after getting back from Charlotte, I was informed by my roommate that I had to leave. I trusted his word because I had never actually signed a lease. It was the kind of surface-level thinking I was keen to making, the kind with no due diligence behind it. The kind of thinking that everything would fall into place. He had used me to avoid his own eviction. I bowed my head in defeat and wrote it up as another loss. Barely two months after moving in, I was packing my shit up and heading back home.

My parents were once again taking the fallout from my decision making, and I had the feeling even they were giving up. I knew they were tired of the run around and constant failure. But despite the surface-level disappointment, they still hung on to hope.

I was only home this time around for a month. That's how long it took for my mom and I to clash heads completely. She was essentially done dealing with me, but her love for her son often overpowered common sense. She was at a dead end but couldn't stop loving me. It was the type of separation that couldn't come naturally for a mother, but it becomes necessary when dealing with a person in active addiction. Soon enough, the cards would play themselves out and the house would win.

I packed my crap into the car yet again and started the drive down I-65 south towards Brentwood. The new place would be an apartment on Edmondson Pike in South Nashville. I found it through Craigslist but had little hope it would work out. This type of traveling became an all-too familiar tale. Benji was once again squeezed into my car with a new destination. He looked worn out and sad. Even he knew I was going the wrong direction.

This nomadic, unpredictable life felt normal by this point. I drank to forget my problems, yet the problems only surmounted.

Alcohol became another glass of water. Just another day to repeat yesterday. I'd wake up hungover, try to remember yesterday, have pangs of regret and guilt, followed by an immense wave of shame. I'd then drink to cover that guilt and continue until I passed out. It was no way to live, but my body relied on it.

I was surprised I got approved for the new place because my credit was completely shot. I sublet from a guy who was moving back to Utah. He was homesick. It seemed like Nashville had chewed him up too. Passing shadows filled the place—by this point maybe it was me.

It had been a few months since the called-off wedding, and I was still trying my best to get over it by getting under people.

Eliana would ask me to dog-sit for a few days while she traveled to New York to see her ex-boyfriend. I told her I'd do it. I figured I could sit over there and drink. At least it would be a different setting. While there, I wondered what the hell I was doing. I wasn't getting paid for the job, and, honestly, I barely knew her. I was a lost person in a stranger's house.

With North pointing South and East pointing West, my moral compass was completely broken. While Eliana was slowly fading, I'd also meet another girl named Kinsley. It was like falling dominos, one after the other. By this point, a sex addiction was now in the picture. It was a true problem. I had grown accustomed to making sure there was always someone else around the corner. I was too scared to be alone, and the dating app made it too easy to meet new people and continually lie and start over. It was both a blessing and a curse. No one had to know my past or underlying issues. All they'd see was a tall artistic guy with a cute black dog and a motorcycle. Those were about the only three things I had going for me.

Being the piece of shit I was, I'd invite Kinsley over while Eliana was gone. For all Kinsley knew, I was dog-sitting for a friend. It made me look like a person who actually had friends. Kinsley and I would have sex in the very bed Eliana and I did just days before. It was a crowning achievement for the biggest low life, but I didn't care. It was just another dirty deed.

I scooted Kinsley out the door knowing I would be picking up Eliana from the airport a few hours later. I was exhausted from keeping the facade and keeping my stories straight. It was exhausting. I approached arrivals with zero fanfare and dropped her off at her house. There was a mutual understanding that whatever the situation was, it would be the last time we'd see each other. And even though it was only a casual relationship, it was yet another person that bit the dust. Aria too, had already left the picture.

As the sun set on the drive home, I knew what tomorrow would bring. I'd wake up early and hope for a ping on my phone. A ping that would only bring in a few more dollars from a Lyft ride. I had no real job and no real hope. I was chasing that next high only to be let down harder the next time.

I pulled into the parking spot and put the car in park with Benji in the back seat. He was leaning against the fuzzy seat with his head down, his eyes still on me. He never took his eyes off me; he hadn't for years. With a heavy head and regretful eyes, I looked at him knowing tomorrow would be no different. It was as if we were having the exact same thoughts.

19

Kinsley

I'd first meet Kinsley in a dingy bar off West End Avenue called Springwater. It's a bar across the street from Vanderbilt and next to the Parthenon. It's a place they call the oldest bar in Nashville and was in fact there during the World's Fair back in the late 1800s. It's a place where the Black Keys and Ke$ha filmed one of their music videos, a bit of information I gladly spilled during our first meeting. Anything to give the impression that I was in.

Springwater had a novelty about it, that old Nashville feel. It was in line with other Nashville staples like Santa's Pub, The Station, and The Nations. Springwater is a place full of characters. People from all backgrounds. People at all stages of life. Attached to the bar stands a greasy lady who sweats in tacos that are strangely good. It's food that fits the midnight taste buds.

It's a place where dusty men talk about the golden days. The history seeps through the torn concert posters and sticks to decades-old bubble gum under the bar. Not many women show up and the ones who do smell like yesterday's decisions. It's a place where several people have overdosed and keeled over beside the toilet. It's a place where people piss on the floor and don't wipe their ass. It's a place that never has towels to wash your hands. It was the perfect place for a first date, right?

I was drinking all afternoon, still swiping left and right on the Bumble app. It was a way to pass the time and find more participants in this fucked-up parade. By the time evening hit, Kinsley sent me a message saying she could meet up that night. I had nothing better to do and there were no other good prospects ringing through the phone, so I figured why not? She seemed very pretty based on her posted photos.

She walked in Springwater wearing a red flowered jumper which contrasted the dark black dress code. She was lovely. She sparkled with a sheen of confidence that exuded around her body. She sat down at an aggressive angle and jumped straight into asking questions, which surprised me. I didn't expect that from such an innocent-looking girl, but I answered all of her questions in a confident drunken stupor. I'd later find out she was grittier than she looked.

Even if I was putting on a show of confidence, for the first time in a long while, I felt comfortable. But I knew if I unloaded everything on her at once, I'd never see her again. And I knew I didn't want that to happen; she was sexy.

Growing up in California had given her an open spirit. Kinsley seemed accepting and didn't prance around on a horse that seemed too big or too small. She had the perfect balance of sugar and spice.

She was getting a little loose so we moved outside to an old diner booth on the back patio. We were both on the same wavelength. She had a 'keep up with me' attitude and that kept my interest peaked. We developed a taste for vodka and decided to go east to the Lipstick Lounge, the gay-friendly bar I always tried to drag Emily to. I knew the same bartenders and clientele would be there—all the people I was trying to avoid since everything with Emily imploded.

We sat on the porch with loose tongues and laughed about nothing. She had a sense of humor that fit perfectly with mine and several drinks later, staring at each other's eyes, she grabbed the back of my head and laid a kiss on me. Her moist, vodka-cranberry colored lips touched mine. They were cold and reminded me that a spark was still possible. The kiss scraped the rust from my heart. It was a perfectly bold move and made me want more. We ended the night together and woke up the next morning with steady headaches. I wasn't sure if I'd see her again, but I got her number in hopes I would. She was a woman I couldn't let fall through my hands.

I'd see her again several days later at the Greenhouse Bar in Green Hills, and this time around would be crazier than the first. I was nervous to see her again. After all, second dates are sometimes awkward. She walked in looking better than the first time; her long, flowing, blonde hair and perfect curves fitting so nicely in her summer dress. We grabbed a cocktail and stepped outside.

I had to continue the act of having my shit together—that meant lying about a myriad of things. I quickly told her I had a master's degree in painting. I sounded smart saying it and knew it would impress her. It wasn't a complete stretch, either. I had the personal paintings to back it up if she decided to do some digging.

By this point lying had become second nature. I would lie about anything, big to small. It was hard keeping track of which fairytale story I told to whom. I woke up every day with a rattled conscience but drowned it with booze to make it feel better. Like all lies do, this fraudulent master's degree would eventually come back and bite me in the ass.

She would tell me a little bit more about her family, which started to sound more like the Kardashians. There were 6 kids including her, and all but one were girls. It was a big family that was full of drama. Kinsley grew up in a busy home and butted heads with her mom growing up. She was the middle child and sounded like the peacemaker of the family, the link between the younger and older sides. We had that in common.

Her dad sounded similar to my own. He was funny and played basketball in college. He was an astute businessman who accumulated a decent amount of wealth which provided for the family. He was patient and kind and always answered phone calls. He was a loving husband who supported his wife. Kinsley would later tell me I reminded her of her dad, but I wasn't sure why. I was a complete mess on the front lines of addiction. It was flattering, but I didn't believe it myself.

Her mom sounded a bit frantic. She was a busy woman, like my own, and ran a marathon years back. She was a nutritionist and a health nut. She sounded like a complex lady with her own unique coming of age story. She got a job as an airline attendant and dabbled into addiction herself. It was the 80s after all. Kinsley had yet to find out about my own, and I refrained from pointing out the correlation between her mom and myself.

I quickly found out Kinsley was a very empathetic person. She worked as a nanny for a wealthy family in Belle Meade and juggled looking after 4 kids. It didn't take long for me to realize that she put her heart into what she did, something I never did professionally. Little did she know I was barely holding onto my own teaching job.

Kinsley was a girl who had mystery to her. People hurt her before, and she had her guard up. She had been exposed to an addict before and knew what came with the territory. The difference was the previous guy was in recovery while I was at the height of addiction and chaos. I think part of her thrived off the apparent excitement that came with active addiction. It was the exact opposite of the dry drunk nature her previous relationship held.

We hung out at the Greenhouse Bar for a bit and then took an Uber back to Lipstick Lounge. It was a place I couldn't seem to leave. This time around, we ran into Owen, whom I hadn't seen since my binger back in December. I had gone off the map, deleted his number, and tried to move forward. But the bar seemed to always align our lives in a similar direction. Owen was in his upper 30s and moved to Nashville from Oklahoma. He grew up with an abusive dad and practically cut ties with the rest of his family. He was a guy, who like me, never seemed to grow up and would be the last person left at the bar before close.

We all hung around the bar for some time and ended the night over at his place. I popped open the back gate and laid eyes on the backyard where I sat, high as a kite on cocaine, as Emily left for the holidays. It was a place I thought I'd never come back to, but there I was and there was Owen, with a bag full of molly. My nose tickled at the thought of snorting a line, and it wasn't long before it was up my nose.

I gave zero shits about catching some sort of bloodborne disease and focused more on the elevated levels of consciousness I was about to experience. With Kinsley already drenched in liquor herself, I figured she wouldn't care. It wasn't long before Kinsley and I were hooking up on Owen's living room couch in the pitch-black space. She was caught up in the unsustainable madness that never seemed to leave me.

We went back to my place as the morning sun rose above Highway 65 heading towards Brentwood. I skipped work, pulled the curtains close in my room, and we slept until noon. She snapped awake, out of the haze, and remembered what happened the night before. I could tell her mind was racing. After such a crazy night, she told me she didn't want to associate with someone who did drugs. I felt a wave of heat spread throughout my body; I could feel a panic attack coming. It was only the second date, but I knew I lost her. I didn't blame her. She wanted a good time, but the night went overboard.

The shutting of the apartment door opened a wave of regret and the familiar feelings I had gotten to know all too well. My addiction had pushed her away quicker than the others. I was positive I'd never see her again. But there was an unexplainable attractiveness to it all. It's a weird push and pull that most alcoholics project. Don't get me wrong—alcoholics may be fucked up, but we're a hell of a good time. We're also pretty convincing. To my surprise she texted me that night saying she'd give me another chance. It would be the first of many, with many highs and lows in between.

She'd come over to my apartment in South Nashville and sit by the pool. I had nowhere else to be and my new roommate, a clueless 21-year-old girl I found on Craigslist, was never home. Her room looked like a trash dump with pizza boxes and White Claws everywhere. I made the mistake of opening her room's door once. That was a big mistake...it smelled like a wet dumpster.

Vanderbilt had hired me to work at their art summer camp, but I quit just three weeks in. It had become too difficult to wake up at the crack of dawn with a pounding head. With no idea of how I was going to pay next month's rent, my chances of this new place becoming a stable home were grim. Maybe the leasing company would extend my due date, but it was wishful thinking. With

eviction imminent, I knew I'd have to come up with a cover story.
More lies.

20

Fiction and Non-Fiction

Kinsley couldn't stop talking about my master's degree. I think she was impressed, and I was equally impressed that I convinced her I had one. She told her friends and eventually her family, putting me deeper in the shitter. I should've thought that one through, but I was incapable of backtracking or keeping my stories straight. I knew what I wanted, and it was her. Kinsley was the whole package. She had a stable job, a faith that grounded her, and was caring, even towards someone as broken as me. The thing was she didn't really know me and would she after all the truths came flooding out? I'd later find out she would.

Eventually a letter showed up on my front door regarding an eviction. They were kicking a dead man, for Christ's sake. I was still scraping bottom by driving for Lyft. It was a job that paid shit but was convenient. And convenience was a killer for me. I could make my own schedule and start drinking whenever I wanted. I'd have a few liquor drinks down the tube and get a ring for a ride. With a buzz, I'd pick people up, drive them to their destination, and forget how I got there. But hell, I just made enough money for my afternoon drinks. I had zero regard for others' safety, and I'm surprised nothing terrible ever happened.

I showed up to eviction court, embarrassed as hell. I sat there amongst others who were there to meet the same fate. We all sat waiting for our case number to be read. I wasn't surprised my roommate didn't show up. I was surprised I even did. I was struck with a large payback and was told my roommate wouldn't face any charges. She was a no show and couldn't be found. I was screwed over for actually having some integrity for once.

I drove back home and called Kinsley to tell her I was evicted. She laughed, a reaction I didn't expect, as I put the blame on my roommate. If she knew the real reason, there was no way she'd talk to me again. After all, why would she want to date a 29-year-old who couldn't even keep up with the most basic of bills?

I proceeded to explain how I'd be moving to a new place off Charlotte Avenue where two drag queens lived. I told her I knew them from Lipstick Lounge and somehow she bought it. It was another confirmation that I could get away with practically anything.

The fact was I was moving back home, again. Kinsley would ask to come over, but I avoided the topic by telling her the place was a mess and my roommates were crazy.

We'd hang out at her place in Bellevue. She had a nice one-bedroom apartment in a swanky complex. There was a pool where we'd drink all day and get sunburnt sitting on the white fold out chairs. It didn't take much for her to get sauced, and she'd play Taylor Swift as we sat next to the fire pit. We'd meet others who lived at the complex, making half-hearted connections that lasted as long as the sun was up.

There was a couple we'd meet that lived across the hall. They were homebodies that crowned themselves the king and queen of the complex. It seemed like they knew everyone and had a dog that Benji would sometimes play with. I acted like I enjoyed their company but only stuck around because the guy had a monthly prescription for Adderall. I used him for that factor alone and once he no longer sold me pills, I threw his company in the trash.

Our first summer together was ending and what started as lust turned to love. There was a connection that seemed to push through all the lies. It seemed like almost every day was an adventure. We'd go to Play and dance, get smashed at Vinyl Tap or Lipstick Lounge, and meander through Nashville's city parks. I was irresponsible in the best way possible, and it fueled a relationship built on fire.

We'd take my motorcycle out at night and wrap our bodies together as we circled the city. There's a part on Highway 40 just past the city where the yellow shine of the streetlights go off and the stars shine down. On the bike it feels like flying. Kinsley loved the feeling of flying. She would stick her arms out like airplane wings and let the air graze the tips of her fingers. I think it brought her closer to God.

We'd go to an open field where fireflies floated and count stars like two high schoolers who found love for the first time. The field became our escape venue. It was just past the place where I proposed to Emily a year before. It became the place where I could rewrite that story, its giant meadow a blank canvas. But in so many respects, I was still the same person. I was a person who would be unable to move forward by staying the same, repeating the same patterns, and downplaying my problems. Kinsley and I were still in the honeymoon phase, and it wouldn't be long till reality dropped right in front of her.

Over the next few months, Kinsley and I became closer than ever, and at times, I almost forgot that the life she thought I lived wasn't true. I had convinced myself that maybe I did have that master's degree in painting, maybe I did live in that house on Charlotte Avenue, and maybe she would never find out just how bad my addictions were. It was a relationship that swayed the lines between fiction and non-fiction. Kinsley was slowly falling in love with a guy who appeared put together but was completely lost. And I was falling in love with a girl I knew I'd eventually hurt.

As the colors of fall settled in, Kinsley found out that I lived with my parents. It was a released burden, and I scrambled to make it up to her. Luckily, I still had some charm, but Kinsley was starting to catch on. We had spent enough time together to figure it out.

21

No Change Nothings

By late November I came across a guy at the Exxon gas station on the corner of Murphy Road and West End Avenue. I was on my way home from Springwater and stopped by that night to grab some beer. Instead, I bought a gram of crystal meth and proceeded to snort it, staying up for three days straight. It made me feel fucking amazing, but I knew going so high meant the fall was going to be sharp.

I was trying to figure out a different career. Sure, I could've gotten another teaching job but how long would that last? With the brainstorming help of my parents, I jumped from insurance underwriter to truck driver to going back to school for some sort of technical trade degree. They were all shots in the dark and had zero chance for lift off. I mean I was high on meth, for Christ's sake. I even attempted to see a career coach, while on meth. Let's just say that didn't pan out.

My sister was getting married in mid-November, and although I was happy for her, it was yet another reminder of how much of a fuck up I was. Kinsley was coming down with me, so it wouldn't be all bad. I convinced my parents I had my drinking together and told myself I'd be taking full advantage of the open bar. On the afternoon I was set to leave, I was sitting on the front porch of my parents' house, trying not to succumb to the piles of hydrocodone I had eaten a few hours before. I managed to open an old safe in the basement with a makeshift rounded bit of cardboard. I was sure I was overdosing. My body heated up, and my vision bounced with black pebbles from blink to blink. Luckily, I also ate some Adderall from my dad's bathroom drawer. I think just maybe that kept my heart beating and my lungs pumping air. Dying on the front porch a day before my sister's wedding was the way I almost went out, but I still didn't stop. I continued to eat Adderall the entire weekend and got absolutely smashed. Of course, my dad found out when we got back and completely lost it. It was getting ridiculous.

December came. It had been an entire year since shit hit the fan with Emily. I was a few weeks into my meth binge and had maybe gotten forty-eight hours of sleep in five days. It was slowly turning my mind into spaghetti sauce, and the chase was getting expensive. At eighty bucks a gram, I couldn't keep the habit up. I'd last a week or two more before the supply ran out. The dealer disappeared, so I stopped... by the grace of God. I probably would have done it till the end, but that wasn't His plan apparently. So, I dialed up the drinking back to high.

I'd hang out with Kinsley on meth, staying up all night and staring at the ceiling, my heart going a mile a minute and trying not to wake her as she slept. I didn't want her to know I was on that shit. I'd wake up in the morning and tell her I couldn't sleep for some unknown reason, but I knew exactly why.

That January, I scored another job teaching at a Nashville elementary school on the north end of town. I was happy I got the job because I needed the money, but I wasn't happy to be back in the classroom. It was once again a job I entered out of necessity. I had to make money—to pay whatever bills I decided were necessary, but also to support my drinking and drug habit.

The elementary school was a rough place with kids who came from poverty. They were cute but had already been through so much; you could see it in the way they looked at you. Some were timid and scared; others were angry and belligerent. They were kids that needed patience and kindness, two things I had very little of. I'd smoke a bowl of weed before heading to work most days and sit at my desk munching down a biscuit I bought at the corner store to soak up my hangover. I'd sit there and dread the start of the first class. I finally had a principal that funded my lessons; if only I made actual lesson plans to use them. I made up plans on the fly and hoped my principal wouldn't come in to observe me. I'd scramble from table to table, putting out crying spells and cleaning up spilled paint cups. By the end of the day, the room was a mess; I didn't bother cleaning up. I was in a rush to get to the liquor store and forget the day.

The paycheck was more than enough to fund my bar bills and liquor store fees. I'd buy expensive bottles and down them in one night. I'd easily spend $100 at the bar and buy drinks for everyone around me. It was a job that fed my addiction perfectly.

I made it a whole year working at the elementary school, but the start of spring in 2020 had a surprising twist for us all. After a tornado completely wrecked East Nashville and destroyed some of my favorite drinking spots, it wasn't long before COVID made an unexpected appearance and brought my problems to an all-encompassing climax.

I hit my 30th birthday when the Covid pandemic was just beginning. I thought I'd never see that age and spent the night having dinner with my parents and Kinsley. I had recently moved back to East Nashville to a small duplex on Andy Street off Litton Avenue. That side of town kept calling me back. I was too proud to stay home and get help. It became harder and harder to understand who I was in the state I was in. I was caving in on myself. The house was within walking distance to a liquor store, Mickeys, and Walden. I pretty much lived alone because the lady I was renting the room from was barely there.

I'd go to the bar and sit there for hours, ignoring texts from Kinsley and testing different drinks as if I was drinking for the taste. I'd sit there, sometimes until closing time, and call out of work the next day without a care. A substitute would never fill my job and the other teachers would have to deal with the absence. I didn't care. It just meant I had a whole day to drink and aimlessly stare at YouTube videos. I got paid to miss work and sent emails saying I was sick. It wasn't a complete lie—I was up all night hunched over the toilet bowl. It was an endless cycle of waking up hungover and making the call on whether to go to work or not. I didn't care if the kids had an art lesson that day. I only cared if I got my fix.

Kinsley recognized what I was doing. By that point, she knew the pattern, but couldn't do much besides make a comment here and there. I'd often lie and tell her I was at work even when I wasn't. We lived close to each other, and I thought the chances of her seeing me walk into the liquor store were high. I'd double check my surroundings and often drive to a liquor store where I knew she wouldn't catch me.

The guys behind the liquor store counter knew my routine and once they saw me walk in, they'd reach for the bottles I liked. They knew what I wanted, and I felt required to buy it. I must've dropped $500 a week at the store. No wonder they greeted me like their friend. They were friends that would take every last penny from me until I passed out on the side of the road foaming from the mouth.

The fraudulent master's degree eventually came out during a heavy night of drinking. I didn't have the courage to tell Kinsley straight because I was a fucking coward. As expected, she retreated, and I didn't hear from her for a week or so. I was confident that was the last nail in the coffin. I remember sitting in my tiny room on Andy Street that night. I felt small. I was bathed in gin and smelled like sin. I was someone I never wanted to be but had become. Fear and anxiety shook me.

Kinsley deserved more. It had been weeks, maybe even months, since I took her on a date. I was incapable of it. My world was surrounded by bottles, smokes, and pills, and I didn't have money for the slightest sign of endearment. Looking back, there were a thousand things I could have done that were free, but I was someone who only cared about me. Me. Me. Me.

Kinsley found hope in a higher power and believed that just maybe, He could get it right. She always said she prayed for me, but those words hit my hard-headed skull with minimal impact. Little did I know that magic was slowly working beneath my human comprehension. Through it all, she held herself up with subtle confidence and was firm in her beliefs. I often wondered why she liked me. I had done everything I could to push her away, but she still stuck around.

I was downing a fifth and more of gin every day at this point. COVID-19 had caused my teaching schedule to go completely virtual. I was drinking behind the camera, teaching kids who were damaged, kids that were starving and beaten, kids whose parents had pennies in their pockets and little hope for the future. I wanted to be there for them, but I was up a never-ending flight of stairs.

I was seeing everything in a blurry haze. Kinsley would get home from nurturing a baby girl, three young boys and then nurture me, a grown man who was broken and in pieces. She was patient and kind, but I resented her for it. She had conviction in things you couldn't see, touch or feel. I wanted what she had. I didn't want to lose her, but I was incapable of loving anyone. Everything in my life was about to fold.

22

When Morning Doesn't Matter

It was a few months into the COVID pandemic, and the fear of the unknown became commonplace around town. No one truly knew what to do with themselves. A lot of people lost their jobs, and everyone was stuck at home. People were struggling, including myself, but I knew exactly how to fill this newly found free time—drink from sunup to sundown. There wasn't one minute in my day where I didn't have a drink by my side.

My new place had a yard where Benji could play. It faced the back of another house and there wasn't much to see. The sky was clear most nights, and I spent a lot of time looking up. *Was God really there?* I felt stuck in the pattern that solidified over the years. My brain and body knew nothing else, and there was no time to recover. My depression was getting a lot worse, and I was encouraged to speak to a psychiatrist. I got the medication, but the alcohol seemed to render it useless. I still took it to trick myself into thinking I was doing something right.

Kinsley still came around, and we hung out on my drinking schedule. We barely did anything she wanted to do. The stay-at-home order was perfectly fostering my addiction. It was the perfect excuse to only move my arms to my mouth, walk to the bathroom and back, or to the fridge. I barely moved for weeks; my online teaching became a forgotten pastime. I assumed it was completely useless teaching art online. *What the fuck was I doing? What was the point?*

My routine consisted of waking up at 7 a.m., sending Kinsley off to her job, and driving to the liquor store by 7:55 a.m... I would wait in the parking lot along with the homeless for the store to open at 8. I became a soulless body with no hope. Kinsley was aware but had different things to worry about. She had to take care of herself.

COVID put a stop to everything 'normal.' I couldn't go sit in a restaurant; I couldn't travel; I couldn't go visit my family; I couldn't go to the grocery store; I couldn't go to work. Come to think of it, it's not like I ever did any of those things in the first place. The world was shut down, just like my ambitions, and at that point, my drinking problem was clearer than water. I was isolated in a city full of thousands.

I had all the time in the world to think about life and how broken peoples' lives had become. It wasn't just me. In a matter of weeks everything was different. No more parking lots full of minions running into Home Goods and Burlington Coat Factory to buy shit they didn't need. It was this previous view from Kinsley's apartment that was the definition of American consumerism. There were no cars on the roads, no lights to be stopped at, no buses to pass. It was as if the things we once cared for no longer mattered. I drove around at night with no one on the road but me. Where did everyone go?

The toilet paper aisle was empty, so I wiped my ass with a shirt. My room was a pigsty and smelled like spilled beer, smoked bowls, and molding juice containers. There was torn artwork across the floor and random scribbles on paper tacked to the wall. I called it art. I was slowly going insane. Delirium tremens, wet brain, and liver damage weren't too far away.

My roommate started to hate me. I couldn't blame her. I was a drunk asshole who ruined the things she bought for the living room and smashed drinking glasses as they slipped from my drunken hands. She'd blow up on me every two weeks when she would stop by.

I talked to my parents once every few weeks. I just didn't feel a need to talk to them. It was a distance that got further away with each passing day. I didn't read anything positive, I didn't move, and Benji was further ignored. I talked to my psychiatrist and told her I was lessening my drinking. She was just one more person I was lying to. I thought she'd never know through a computer screen, but I'm sure it showed.

That summer, I'd have a Fourth of July party with a handful of people. With the amount of alcohol I had on hand, you'd think fifty people were showing up; I ended the night telling two guys to get the fuck out. I'm still not sure what they did, but whatever it was pissed me off.

It was no surprise that Kinsley was getting even more worried about my habits. She knew I was drinking while teaching kids through Zoom classes, she knew I went straight to the bar after I ended the last class early, and she knew that I wasn't going to get any better. Unlike my parents, she saw first-hand the current unraveling of the David she thought she knew.

I was continuing to make my rounds to my usual stops where I'd come across Owen. There were other shadow dwellers as well. Douglas was an older man, with a lazy right eye stuck in the corner pocket. At his age, he was still blowing cocaine and drinking every day, something I saw for my own future. He was a guy who was there physically but never mentally, and he had drugs, so conversation never mattered. He'd hang around Kinsley and me, and we'd prod him about what he did for work. We never got a clear answer, a common consensus amongst the people that frequented the spots where I went. There was also Eric, a female who was transitioning to a male that hit on Kinsley behind my back. He, too, walked around the bar with the goodies I was seeking. It wasn't hard to notice when he was packing. He wore a black backpack on his wiry shoulders which sent a signal to the hordes that he was ready to unload.

As October 2020 approached, Kinsley and I called it quits. There were too many missed calls, deleted texts, and sketchy outings to trust me anymore. I had shown up at her house shirtless and strung out one cold morning and banged on her door until she answered. Living so close meant unannounced visits were easy.

I went back on Bumble to find someone else to fuck. One day I was crying over losing Kinsley, and the next, I was looking for someone to get on top of. It was a disgusting pattern that would break me months later, but for now, I let it fly.

After buying mushrooms from a random neighbor and spending the night being laughed at while trying to play a board game, I called up a girl named Audrey to hang out with during Halloween. It was a holiday that marked the beginning stages of the final showdown between me and myself.

I'd sleep with Audrey that Halloween night, get chlamydia, and wake up to a phone call from Kinsley. *What in God's name could she still want with me?* I answered in the bathroom while Audrey was still in bed, and she laughed about how I couldn't get her out of my house. Apparently, Kinsley also slept with a stranger the previous night and was also struggling to separate herself from the mistake. We both were dealing with our situation in unhealthy ways. How could I be mad at her? I had done far worse.

The fucked-up happenings of Halloween brought Kinsley and I back together. Thanksgiving passed with little fanfare, and as Christmas approached, there was no end in sight for the COVID pandemic. *What the hell happened the past year?*

The fact that the world was ending seemed like a fitting end to my life story. I could finally go down in the blaze of drunken glory that I started on so many years ago. I finally had an excuse for drying out into a raisin and folding like a day-old newspaper. This was what God had planned for my life. I was at least complying with the agenda. My body was slowly dying. I was throwing up almost every night, mostly orange liquid and stomach acid. I pooped yellow goo with brown mucus spots and blood, and my lower back was constantly in pain. I hadn't solidly pooped in months and could barely hold down the fast food I was eating. My body was beginning to show signs of shutting down.

I didn't have the energy to think about pursuing help—not that I would. I didn't have the patience to sit in an AA meeting, talk to a therapist, or enter rehab. I didn't have the determination to fix the problem I had gotten myself into. It was much easier to accept my fate. It was my fault, and no one else was around to carry the load. Unsurprisingly, Kinsley was once again distancing herself after weeks of being unable to sleep next to a guy whose body would muscle spaz throughout the night. There were many nights she'd put her ear up to my mouth to make sure I was still breathing. She started to assume I wouldn't wake up.

There were further rumblings of roommate issues. A new girl moved into the room next door. COVID destroyed most relationships; Skylar's was no different. She needed a room fast, so I agreed as one last act of kindness before I left earth. She started moving her stuff in the next morning. She seemed nice, and we tried to avoid each other the best we could in that small house.

The thing was, I never got along with roommates, so why would this situation be any different? There was no chance of it working out, but I wouldn't be there much longer. I knew I'd either get kicked out or kicked off the planet. The physical ailments would take me soon enough, and I'd cuddle Benji for one last time. Maybe I wouldn't wake up in the morning.

I'd spend that Christmas alone in my room, ignoring phone calls from my parents. I'd sit there alone all day, drinking straight from the bottle and crying my eyes out. I'd sit there with my back to Benji and head down. I was shot and my brain was falling apart. I was struggling to get a grip on reality. By this point, the conversation between Kinsley and me was mostly filled with arguments. She was getting maxed out on babysitting a grown man. My addiction had its full arms around me and any control I thought I had was completely gone. The months were numbering.

23

Numbering

It was late January in 2021, and snow had been falling heavily for five days. School was out, even virtual school. Unfortunately for Kinsley, she still had to go to work. The families she worked for struggled without her, and she needed any excuse to get out of the house and away from me. It was only a matter of time before my liver would give out. I felt unfettered. I had moved into Kinsley's house after getting kicked out of my place on Andy Street earlier that month. Kinsley couldn't bring herself to leave me in the state I was in. Slamming doors and the sound of her crying put me to sleep. Kinsley was tortured with uncontrollable grips of anxiety. The source: me.

I had gotten home from the hospital a week before after driving over to my old place on Andy Street to pick up some leftover mail. After stuffing old Cookout french fries into the mailbox out of spite, I turned around and made the short drive back home. Halfway there, a strong pressure collapsed on my stomach, then a numbing feeling crept up my chest, around my shoulders, down my arms, and to the tips of my fingers. I couldn't feel anything, and my blood pressure started to fluctuate from high to low. My head got light, I started to sweat, and I panicked. I jumped out of the car and fell to the ground murmuring to myself, "Not now, dear God." All the damage I caused to my body was catching up with me. The drinks, drugs, lack of nutrition, and sleep finally hit me. I was convinced I was going to die there, behind the Tennessee Quick Cash building. I thought of all the wrongs I never made right. All the people I squeezed dry. All the people I lied to and cheated on. My parents whom I ignored and pushed aside. *How would God judge me once I approached the pearly gates?* I wasn't ready to die with such guilt and shame. I was going to die a broken man. I sat on the concrete clutching my stomach, scared to death and unable to move.

Two nearby construction men saw me struggling and ran over. They were two burly, rough and tough dudes, men I never thought would help me. They ended up being my two angels. They talked to me and kept my attention off the pain in my body. The medics arrived, strapped me to the stretcher and put me in an ambulance. All the while, Benji sat in the passenger seat of my car. He'd be driven home by one of the construction workers while I was wheeled off to the emergency room.

On the ride to the hospital, I felt like I couldn't breathe. The pain in my chest and pressure on my stomach didn't let me. They wheeled me through the hospital, the fluorescent lights passing above me like some time warp to the afterlife. It felt like a movie, and I faded in and out of awareness. I didn't know what was happening to me. Doctors came into the room, one after the other. They took my blood pressure, pulled my blood, checked my eyes, and put IVs into my arms. I was wheeled to an MRI machine where light spun around me like a fucked-up episode of Star Trek. I threw up all over the nurse next to me, and she cursed at me telling me to suck it up. She wasn't wrong. I'd have to if I was going to walk out of there in the flesh and bones suit I rolled in on.

I'd sit in that white-walled room for the next eight hours, staring at the ceiling with nothing else to do but think. I was alone, and I didn't know where my cell phone was. No one knew I was there. *Was I going to die alone in an empty hospital room?* I thought about my body and how much torture I put it through. I thought about all the wires and the beeping of the machine by my side. Was this really it? Was this really how I wanted to go... at thirty years old? The doctor would look me straight in the eye and say, "You are an alcoholic, and this disease will kill you if something doesn't change." It was enough to scare the shit out of me.

I hadn't been able to call anyone all day, and I knew Kinsley would worry. Through all the mental pain I put her through, she still loved me. I knew she'd see Benji in the backyard and wonder where I was. *Did she think I finally took my own life, or did she think I was out on Broadway getting smashed one last time?* I felt guilty for being where I was—first-hand repercussions of my habitual drinking and drugging.

The doctor had given me the grave warning. So naturally, I checked out of the hospital, walked ten miles home, and told myself I'd continue to wear my hospital band as some sort of promise to myself to never end up there again. It was a short sign of sobriety that only lasted one week. It wasn't long before I was driving straight to the liquor store. Crazy, am I right?

During my time in the hospital, Kinsley was convinced I took my life and was already running around the thought in her head of how she would tell my parents. How could she give them the news that no parent wants to hear? I was beginning to go insane and knew an asylum was on the horizon. Did those still even exist?

A few days later, I was sitting in Kinsley's guest room as she went to work. The blinds were torn in half and there was piss in bottles laid across the floor and shoes scattered throughout the room. There was Sour Patch on the walls and crushed chips in every corner. I had become too lazy to walk to the bathroom and too embarrassed to show my face. I would wake up on the bed sideways, bowls with spit and vomit next to me. I looked like a disheveled piece of shit.

My back was constantly aching, and my eyes sunk with each passing day. My laptop played the same songs on YouTube. It was a sick repeat of the day before. Benji no longer slept in my room, spending his days on Kinsley's bed instead. He was trying to find some sense of peace and cried at my closed door when he had to use the bathroom. I ignored him and stared at the wall.

My feet were dark purple; it hurt to walk anywhere. The rising sun that once brought hope no longer had that shine. Alone in a dark house, I sat knowing there was no going back. I was stuck; I failed. I failed myself; I failed my family; I failed Kinsley; I failed Benji; I failed the students I was still somehow teaching. I felt like I had no other reason to live.

I was gone.

I was a prisoner in my own mind. My soul was lost. My life meant nothing, a sick game. I wouldn't see loved ones in heaven because I sinned too much to be forgiven. The shame I felt was too great to live with anymore. I would no longer experience the loving embrace from my mom and dad, no longer hear the sound of chirping birds in the morning breeze or feel the brisk air hitting my chest as I rode my motorcycle. I had taken all these things for granted.

I knew I needed to get help, but I was scared of failure, of letting people down. But how much longer did I need to scrape the bottom? I couldn't take much more.

There'd be nothing waiting for me in the afterlife. I'd be a ghost, a distant memory that would soon be forgotten. My stamp on the world would be lost and the return address would bleed off the side. There would be nothing left to write about. *Just let me sleep*, I thought. Maybe I wouldn't wake up. I'd go without saying goodbye. I wouldn't be missed. I had done nothing to deserve it.

24

Loud

It wasn't just me who was unraveling; Kinsley, too, was beginning to succumb to the stress of living with an alcoholic. Every day was filled with verbal fights, and I was the original catalyst for it all. The walls of her house were cracking.

I soon quit my teaching job before they inevitably pulled the trigger. I wanted to beat them to the punch. I had ended too many classes early, and I'm sure the parents could guess the source of my slurred speech just outside the edge of the Zoom frame. I had given up months before and was surprised I even made it that far. The gin was winning.

In a hungover state of mind, I sent one email saying, "I quit." It was a kick in the face to the principal who hired me. She hired me with the hopes that I could develop into a useful and effective teacher. But I let them all down—the kids, my peers, my boss. With my health on the line, the job that I kept for a decent paycheck no longer seemed as important.

My book of wrongs was thick. I'd be labeled an alcoholic for the rest of my life. I'd be the poster boy for the one who tried and failed. I was someone who was heavily influenced by the people I surrounded myself with. If they were doing a shot, I was doing a shot. If they were going to another bar, I was going to another bar. If they wanted to stay up late, I would stay up late. It didn't matter if I had work the next day or if Kinsley wanted me to come home. I was a 'yes man' to all the wrong things. The old saying, 'you are who you hang around,' became all too clear. What my mom and dad had been telling me for years was true, but I had brushed them off.

I had been in contact with a girl named Summer whom I met while on a Sunday drinking campaign. She was with another blonde friend, and we launched into a conversation by her showing me a naked picture of herself. It was a strange way to introduce yourself, but I didn't think twice about it. She came down from Chicago for the weekend and was ending her drinking binge with one last capstone. She told me she had tripped acid the day before and done a handful of other drugs. Was this the perfect match that I needed? I thought, Well, *yes*. I was still thinking about the possibility of getting laid by yet another person, despite living in Kinsley's home.

Summer was the perfect contradiction to Kinsley. Her friend beside her was a porn star, and I had a sneaking suspicion she was in the game too. We smoked a bowl of weed in her Tesla, a sick sign to me that debauchery must pay off. We exchanged numbers and I became convinced I had to drive up to Chicago to see her. Of course, I raised the question: what lie could I tell Kinsley to get out of town? As dysfunctional as our relationship had become, she was always there. Going to Chicago would just be a little jaunt. She'd never find out, right?

I ignored Kinsley like usual and had weird flashes of sitting in our field. Blurry moments of swerving on the highway. Phone calls from unknown callers and Benji cowering in the corner. My knuckles were bleeding. I had been kicked out of several bars and told never to come back. No worries, I wasn't coming back from anything.

I was on the verge of a mental meltdown. After a full day of drinking, I made my way back to Kinsley's house. I jerked into her front yard with a quick stop and kicked a few liquor bottles out of the way to get out of the car. My car reeked of weed and cigarettes.

Unfortunately for Kinsley, she was home. She begrudgingly opened the door and I stormed in. She yelled at me to get out; funny, she thought I would actually listen. I stumbled straight to the room I was staying in and slammed the door. I yanked the blinds hard, snapping them clean off and threw my shoes at the wall. I was a belligerent asshole. I locked the door so she couldn't get in and sat there drinking straight from the bottle as she banged on the door. After a short time, I cracked the door and she reached for my open bottle of gin. I yanked it back and quickly closed the door, catching her foot in the process. The devil was winning, and it wouldn't be long before I was all his. Eventually the banging and pleading at the door stopped and I laid on the bed, my hand clenching the bottle.

My phone soon rang, and I ran out to my car and locked the door. It was the girl I met from Chicago. We were a minute into our conversation when Kinsley stomped outside and pounded on the window. I looked at her with straight disgust. I was a vile human being and doing everything I could to piss her off. Of course, I didn't know how good I had it.

Summer asked, "Is that your girlfriend?"

I reluctantly answered yes, and she hung up the phone. That fling was over just about as fast as it started, and I buried myself deeper in the hole I was already in. I mean, how much deeper could I go?

Kinsley ran back in the house, and for the first time ever, she called my mom and opened up about what was going on. She had been dealing with me alone. She had no one else to talk to. Thirty minutes later, my parents showed up and I was completely out of my mind. I called Kinsley a bitch and gave her a smirk of disgust. I was a shell of a person, and my soul had solidified in shame and guilt.

I stormed down towards the bottom of the hill, the cold air creating a thin trail of smoke with every hot puff from my broken chest. I took cover behind a rundown building, laying there in the fetal position with tears streaming down my bumpy face. As my cheek hit the gravel, the images of the past eleven years ran across my vision. Images of the people I hurt, scoured, and soured. Images of Kinsley, the person I said I loved, but continually pushed away. I saw a kid at eighteen who just finished high school and looked forward to the coming future. I saw a boy who never became a man. And I saw my dog Benji, who always looked at me with hopeful eyes.

I laid on that cold ground for an hour and shivered from top to bottom as the night air settled in. I knew my parents and Kinsley were just up the hill. They were still there waiting for the kid to come back home. Waiting for his soul to be restored. This would be the last rock bottom I would hit.

A subtle voice in the back of my head told me to get up and walk back home. I would later know what that voice was. It was God. I forced myself to stand up, crumbs of dirt falling off the top of my head, and stumbled back up the hill. For the life of me, I couldn't believe how or why they were still there. It was the unconditional love that I didn't deserve.

We approached each other and I looked at all of them with a mix of sadness, horror, disgust, and shame. Somehow, they convinced me to get in the car. For the last time, I'd go back to my parents' house. The eleven-year party was over. It was time to go home.

I woke up the next morning with a sense of urgency. The voice that always told me yesterday didn't matter told me that tomorrow could be better. As long as I didn't drink that day, I could fulfill the hope for tomorrow. It was like God kicked me and gave me one last kiss of life. It was time to get help. I had experienced near death... I had barely survived... enough was enough. I clearly saw that changes had to be made but addressing this addiction had been the mountain I could never seem to start climbing. I had struggled with addiction my entire adult life. Addiction to drugs, alcohol, sex, and often, change. It was either help or the asylum. I was going to hurt myself. Talking to Kinsley about purchasing a gun just days before showed an intention to end this sorry life of mine.

Who was this person looking back at me in the mirror? It wasn't me. I needed professional help. I needed faith in something. I had lost it all, lost everything. It was either sobriety or an early death. It was time to throw in the towel.

I was afraid of what I'd do without a drink. Questions swirled in my head.

How would I have fun without a drink?
How would I make new friends without a drink?
How do I break a habit that had become so ingrained in me?

How would I forgive myself for everything that I had done?

How would I become a new person and forget the old?

What would I do on the weekends when everyone was out on the town?

How would I fill in the gaps of boredom and reach that nice soothing liquid satisfaction of falling asleep?

Was I even capable of being fixed?

I was unable to believe I could change.

But just like before, my mom and dad wouldn't give up on me. They couldn't stand aside and see me fail. I had done them dirty for so long, and I couldn't understand why they wouldn't let go. How did they love me so much? What had I done to deserve this?

Kinsley didn't want to see me anymore, and I understood why. She saw the shadow that was cast over me, and the demons that lingered over my shoulder. She told me she loved me, but she couldn't help me anymore. She couldn't watch me kill myself. She needed to look after herself. She needed to get a handle on her own stress and anxiety. She needed to heal… and I needed to let her.

She looked at me as if she never knew me. She looked at me with shivering bones. She feared for her future, and I feared for mine. I was tired of hurting people. The fear of failure overwhelmed me, but I was going to push myself through the doors of rehab. I'd look at people who might relate to me. But what did they know about what I'd been through? I'd soon find out they related a lot.

25

Entering an Unknown

I approached the inpatient facility sick as a dog, my heart palpitating in odd rhythms. I fell to the floor right before the building's entrance because I could barely walk. Luckily, the nurse helped me to my feet and walked me through the doors to the waiting room. With my mom next to me, we sat in the patient intake waiting area. There were other characters who had already been there for a few days coming to the counter to use their cell phones. You could only use a cell phone a handful of times throughout the week. It was their way of having the patients focus on their rehabilitation. It's embarrassing to admit, but that rule scared me. I knew I would be isolated, but I didn't know my contact with the outside world would be so limited.

While waiting in the lobby, an older man sitting across from me who looked like he lived several lives before looked over at us and said, "Don't focus on the people around you, just listen to the counselors." That advice became truer than ever in the coming weeks. My mother looked at me and said she was so proud of me and that I was making the best decision I could ever make. She was happy to have professionals take the lead in my recovery. I honestly still wasn't sure if I could conquer my addiction. I was only hours into this decision, and the addictive voice in the back of my head was constantly trying to talk me right out of the building. It was the voice I gave into for years, but this time, I was hell-bent on shutting it down. There was no way I was going back because if I did, I knew it meant almost certain death.

I handed in my few belongings like my cell phone and wallet and gave my mom a long hug. A large part of me wanted to succeed in rehab for her, but this time, I was mostly doing it for myself. I walked back to the medical intake and stripped off my clothes behind a curtain so they could check if I was bringing any contraband in. I guess some people decide to put the last of their goodies up their ass or something. They took my weight and blood pressure, then walked me back to a room I would call home for the next month.

The door closed behind me, and I burst into tears. This was really happening, I was getting actual help for the first time, but the sound of the thick wooden door shutting felt like the locking of a prison gate. I felt alone because, well, I was. This would have to be conquered by me and me alone. It was a fact that I had avoided for years. I used to lean on girlfriends, family, and strangers to fix my problems in the past. No more.

The room was sparsely furnished. There was a twin-size bed, a small bedside table, an empty wooden cabinet for clothes (that I thought housed a TV), and a lamp. I laugh at myself now for thinking I could breeze by those thirty days by watching Netflix. I really had to entertain myself the old-fashioned way. I laid on the bed, pulled a thin fuzzy blanket over me and stared at the ceiling. I could almost feel the sweat that was left behind. There were scuff marks on the side of the bed, probably from half- drunk patients who hadn't quite made it to the mattress.

How many people before me laid in this bed and how many saw it through?

Were they still sober beyond these gates?

Had they re-entered the torment of addiction?

My body was still in immense pain and begging for a drink.

I strengthened my resolve. It was me who had to find happiness. It was me who had to beat this. At that particular time, it felt impossible. In the bed-side table was a Bible, one that would typically be found in your roadside motel, a blank notepad and a pen. It was as if God was saying, "Open me and you shall find the way." I was still closed off to that message.

I soon heard my name over the speaker that commanded, "David, time for your meds." I was on their schedule now, not mine. I was on God's time, not mine. I was no longer able to do whatever the hell I wanted. It really upset me, and my brain once again tried telling me this was all just a stupid idea. I was never going to get better.

I walked down the hallway, past open doors with other inmates that just arrived. Some looked better than others, but most of them just walked around in a scared daze. All of our tools of escape were taken away from us, and we looked around at one another, unable to figure out what to do with ourselves. It was sad to see and even more sad looking at myself. It was then and there I realized how dependent I had become on the bottle. I really didn't know what to do with myself.

I sat down in front of the medicine counter and was handed a cocktail of pills. It was a combination of depression, nausea, and pain medicine. To me, the Vicodin was the most important one. In my sick mind, I thought of that as a win. I knew what pain killers would do—they would get me high. I gladly took that one down with an easy gulp. I walked back to my room and took a shower to be somewhat presentable for dinner.

There were some people smoking cigarettes in the gazebo, and I walked outside to strike up a conversation. I didn't want to be alone and figured I needed to make some 'friends' during my time there. We sat in a circle, and they asked me what I was in for. It was like they were sizing me up. I stated a flurry of things and they proceeded to tell me what drugs they had been on. It was a sick competition to see who had gotten closest to the gates of hell. Most of them had been to rehab before; this was their third or fourth time around the block. *Man, I want this to be the first and only trip around this fucked-up summer camp,* I thought to myself. I heard horror stories before and knew relapse was possible, but I didn't want that to be me. I didn't want to experience this shit all over again. I had only been there for two hours at this point. They gave me some words of encouragement, but I knew not to trust them too much. They had already done this before and failed. I really wasn't looking for their advice.

An older man came out into the gazebo and introduced himself to us. He was close to my dad's age and couldn't even hold a fork at dinner because his withdrawal shakes were so bad. He was a nice guy who looked at me like I was his son, and we struck up a conversation on our way to the dining hall.

The campus was pretty and set up like a small college. It had a gym and workout room, but those were closed due to COVID. It had a chapel and an auditorium and a few walking paths that ran alongside the Cumberland River. It was the start of spring and leaves were starting to blossom from the branches. It felt fitting for a change in lifestyle, but the grip of my addictive thought pattern snatched every ounce of hope that fluttered to my mind. My body was still locked in and telling me I couldn't do it.

It felt isolating, but oddly comforting not being the only fucked-up person in a room. We got to the cafeteria and lined up like elementary schoolers on taco salad day. Eating was about all there was to look forward to and the others told me the food was actually quite good. It was all you could eat, after all. I got my food and looked around at the playground of people, an array of backgrounds and ages. People in their teens to people that could be my granddad. People that looked like they were going to fall off their seats and people hunched over the table. People that were dazed on meds and people that had been there several weeks and looked much healthier than the rest. What we all had in common was that we were there to get better. It was sad to think that half of them wouldn't make it through—statistics didn't lie. Doubts about myself continued to strike my mind.

I sat down at a random table of people and the competition continued. There were mostly sad stories about people who had tried and failed rehab before. Stories about wives who left them, kids who cut off contact, endless hospital visits. I sat down with my own racing thoughts. I was missing my family and Benji. I wondered what they were doing, but I knew they were happy I was locked away. They didn't have to worry about me driving drunk and killing someone, or crumbling into a psychotic episode. I wondered what Benji was doing and if he missed me. He had been with me through so much, and I had never been away from him for more than two weeks at a time. He was my black furry angel who looked after me. Maybe I put too much pressure on him, too.

I wrapped up dinner and walked alone back to the living quarters. My thoughts raced. This would be the first time in months I didn't drink all day. I was worried I'd have a seizure and fall off my bed. However, there would be nurses that would walk in every few hours to check on me, and I'd have to stumble down the ghostly hallway to take more meds.

The Vicodin knocked me out pretty well, but I still had awful night terrors and sweat doused the mattress. The detox process had started. My body was praising hallelujahs through every pore, yet my brain still craved a drink. It's a very weird experience to have that battle happening inside of you and recognizing it. It was a self-awareness I forgot long ago.

After being woken up by the nurse four or so times, it was finally morning. I woke to a new day, scared as hell. I thought I'd at least feel a little better, but my shaky hands told a different story.

26

Slight Detour

I sat at the counter to take another round of meds and knew I'd be a zombie all morning after doing so. At least I'd be high and wouldn't feel much. That felt like a good compromise in my head. I went back to my room, took a shower, changed, and tried to write in the sketchbook I brought. It was a sketchbook I wrote in before and tore pages out of—a reminder of trying and failing. I went out to the gazebo where I sat the day before.

There were many faces wearing similar expressions. Most didn't sleep well, and one was even jealous I was given Vicodin to ease the detox process. He told me he sat in his car smoking the last of his drugs before entering the facility. Another guy said he guzzled the last of his alcohol before dragging himself in. I wasn't that bad... or was I? Either way, it didn't do well to compare.

I walked to breakfast with the old man I met before. We talked about his family and wife who were supportive. He had been to rehab before and was adamant on wishing this to be my first and only time. Even though he was someone to lean on, I felt extremely lonely. I missed the people outside the gates.

After breakfast, the loneliness became too much to bear, and I broke down on a bench in the center of campus. I was scared and simply didn't know how to do this. I didn't necessarily want to drink, but it had been a crutch for.me for so long. I was living life sober, and time was creeping by... at a snail's pace.

I didn't know what to do with myself and cried just because I could. It felt like I was back at Davidson basketball camp as a young child who simply missed his parents. But here, I couldn't even call home. I was stuck between the drunk me and the sober person that I could become. I was by myself, inside myself.

I sat on the bench crying as the morning sun rose above the glowing hills across the Cumberland River. People walked by but didn't say anything to me. It was normal to see people breaking into pieces there. I sat there and decided to leave. It was a decision I knew would have implications. My mom and dad would probably think, *Oh my God, he already gave up.*

I knew this decision didn't mean I was giving up. I knew this decision wasn't me throwing in the towel. After all, I had already made it almost twenty-four hours and was feeling just a little bit better. But the fear of failure still hung over me, and the devil inside was constantly talking me into quitting my goal. The habits that became muscle memory were thrown into unusual new thought patterns.

I would check out of the facility and take a taxi to my parents' house. I knew disappointment was waiting for me there.

My parents' house looked the same when I arrived. They still had the same waving seasonal flag, the nicely watered flowers, and the well-manicured grass. The house was the same and so was I. I had left less than twenty-four hours ago to change my life and showed right back up on their doorstep. I looked through the three small windows at the top of the wooden door to see if my dad was sitting at his spot on the couch. It was the place I could always find him watching whatever sport was on the television for the day. I turned the knob and prepared my already weak body for a verbal whiplash of worry. I walked four steps, the floor creaking below me. *Was no one home?* Maybe they were already out celebrating my exit from their lives. I wouldn't blame them. I'd be celebrating, too, following the hell I put them through.

I turned the corner to the living room to see my dad approaching me from the kitchen. I'll never forget the look on his face. He looked stunned but had hope in his eyes. The first thing he said was, "Well, what is our next plan of attack?" To everyone else except my dad, it seemed like I had given up on rehab. But my dad was still the man who knew there would be a solution. He was still the dad who wasn't giving up on me. It was the perfect response in a confusing moment that seemed to have no rationale. And although I was still feeling doubtful, he gave me that bit of confidence I needed to continue to push forward.

We sat down on the backyard porch and discussed my options. I still wanted help and knew the only solution would be outpatient treatment. However, COVID-19 made almost all outpatient programs go virtual. I had taught virtually for almost a year and was under the impression that if it didn't work for my students, why would it work for me? But I figured, why not? It was the only option at that point, and I simply had to do it. With no current job commitment and a deep desire to heal, there weren't any barriers in my way.

Prior to committing to rehab, I had signed a lease for a new apartment. It would be waiting for me to move into once everything settled. But being at the new apartment by myself scared me. I didn't want to be alone with my thoughts which could, at that time, sway me in *any* direction. Vulnerability typically led to the drinking trap. My dad told me that I needed to stay at their house. Unlike the many times before where I treated their house like an addict's playground, I'd now treat it like a SAT test center. I made the phone call back to the rehab facility and told them I wanted to do the outpatient program. They set me up to start the following day.

That night, laying in the guest room bed, I really wasn't sure if I made the right decision to leave. I could feel the doubters floating around me. The heavy load of the attic room just above me weighed down on my chest. Just a few months before, I was up there giving up on life, drowning it with whatever substance I could find. But that day felt different. I was giving it up, *I knew it.*

I opened the Big Book I got from the facility to page one. Searching for what, I'm not sure, probably some clarity or encouragement. Maybe, just maybe, I would find it within the blue-lined Bible for alcoholics. Why not? It was simply worth the shot.

Reading the first few pages was like reading my very own mind. What they described was almost identical to the way I was living my life. The book was written nearly one hundred years ago, yet the addict's condition hadn't changed a bit. The daily decisions, the loss of hope and relationships, the empty pockets and promises, and the habitual repeat of the merry-go-round were no different. It was the first time I was open enough to realize that what I had was a disease that had been around since the beginning of man. There was no reason to cower in the corner out of embarrassment.

There were words of encouragement and glimmers of success, but it was clear that it wouldn't be easy. Many had tried and failed before because they didn't want to give up the bottle. I was an alcoholic long before I called myself one, and my self-will would not be enough to conquer this dilemma. I found the words comforting but daunting. It seemed that giving up control of my own life was the first step in the process. Right then and there, I decided my own will power wasn't enough. I'd have to stop and completely change the way I was living and stop trying to manage my problems on my own accord.

I would never be able to drink again. Not in a few weeks, not in a few months, and not in a few years. I'd have to give up my old way of living and learn a completely new one. I simply had to let go.

I woke up early the next day, made my way to the dining room, and logged into the computer. Papa, my last living grandparent at ninety-one years old, was visiting, and I didn't want to burden him with what I was about to undertake. It felt good being back in a familiar place, and the environment I once wrecked took on a different tone. I was glad he was visiting. It was another good reminder of why I was making the commitment. His presence reminded me of the last few years I spent with Nanny. She would come to visit, but I'd be too busy figuring out my plans for the night. I'd be too drunk or high to remember any of the last few conversations we had, and to make it worse, I was high out of my mind at her funeral. I didn't talk or make some sort of remembrance, focused instead on what alcohol I was going to consume that night. Not only had I wasted my own life, I had wasted my time with others.

My camera turned on and I could see my counselor on the other end of the screen. He was a bald, bearded guy with glasses and to my chagrin, looked like he knew what he would be talking about. I had been a little worried he'd be a prick with no real-life experience, but that didn't feel like it was the case. We went over the normal intake questions. *When was the last time you used? How much were you drinking? Did you have any thoughts of suicide? What was your drug of choice? Why are you seeking treatment?* It was easy to answer all of them; I didn't hold anything back. I had nothing else to lose after all.

He looked at me through the computer screen with a gaze that read, *I hope he can do it.* Doubts continued to seep in about how well treatment would transfer through a computer. He reassured me and told me, "Treatment is what you make it. Just focus on the day, or even just the hour if necessary." This is where I first heard the phrase, "One day at a time." I would cling to this statement, especially during my first thirty days.

After the first hour of intake, the rest of the group joined in. It was mostly what I expected and reflected a similar scene to what I saw in person. All sorts of backgrounds, ages, and a wide range of stories that I thought were worse than my own. We each did a check-in, which basically meant we went down a list of pre-typed questions. These included rating your depression, anxiety, and urge to drink. We went through a list of post-acute withdrawal symptoms (PAWS) like lack of appetite, loss of sleep, irritability, using dreams and many more. I pretty much answered all of them in the high category. Yet others, who had been in the program for a week or two were already answering to a much lesser degree. I wanted what they had.

They had a certain glow and confidence about them, and they talked through the questions that were asked with such ease. There was no hesitation. There were no thoughts of lying or stumbling on sugar-coated words. They spoke honestly, something I hadn't done for years. It was contagious just looking at them. And although it was through a computer screen, I felt connected to something greater than myself. God was working within me.

The group ended at noon. I shut my computer screen and returned to reality. I still had half the day to find something to do.

Staying busy would be one of the hardest parts of the sobriety process. I knew once 4 p.m. rolled around, I would want a drink. It was an easy way to kill time in the past and would ease the transition from sunlight to darkness. I started to realize I couldn't just log off the computer without a plan, otherwise the creeping thoughts of drinking and using drugs would surely win. I had to write down a list of things I would do to fill my time. I made sure the list was too long, essentially making it impossible to complete every task for that particular day. Every minute had to have a place. Doing this also made sure I was too tired to even think about using. It was a strategy that started to work.

Night time was especially hard because that's when my body would physically crave a drink, not just my mind. It would sweat as if crying for one last go on the roller coaster, and the body aches made me feel like I just ran a marathon. My physical responses showed just how sick my body had become. Additionally, I'd have the worst dreams. Dreams of snorting heroin or driving drunk and crashing into an unknown car. They were terrifying, and I'd snap awake with odd heart palpitations. My body was still letting go of all the toxins.

I had driven drunk almost every day for years and was lucky I never killed myself, killed someone else, or been arrested and thrown in jail. I only had one close encounter with a DUI while living in Boone. But after passing the Field Sobriety test and still blowing a .20, the cop allowed my friend to drive me home. Luck was the only explanation for a clean outcome. I would lay in bed at night, reading the Big Book, and look at the ceiling just hoping for another 24 hours. The one day at a time mantra was keeping me sober.

Others in the group hadn't been so lucky. There was a lady who lost her kids through the Department of Human Services and another guy whose wife just left him. There was another guy who was arrested for a DUI and another who was weaning herself off fentanyl. I came to realize I had more in common with these people than what was different about us. We all lied every day, almost every hour. We all stole to support our habits. We all cheated on our girlfriends, boyfriends, husbands, and wives. And we all scraped bottom multiple times before winding up in the rehab room.

Days four and five went by with a similar routine and thought pattern. I would wake up from a terrible night's sleep, log into the computer, talk about the shit person I was, log off, and frantically figure out what to do with the rest of the day. It helped that my dad was there. He kept me busy and out of my mind. I'd ride with him to do simple tasks like going to Walgreens, dropping off a lamp to get repaired, taking bike rides, or working in the yard. I called him the Principal of Rehab School as a joke because he made sure I wasn't too far out of sight. If I left to run a quick errand, he'd call every five minutes to make sure I didn't stop at the corner store.

Surprisingly, Papa also played a key role in my recovery, even though he had no idea what I was going through. He always wanted to hang out, take a walk, or simply take a drive. He liked riding around in the passenger side, looking around, and just talking to me. It was his way of showing he cared. It was also his way of venting about how much he missed Nanny. I didn't blame him. He had been married to her for well over fifty years and was now alone in the world they both conquered together. His strength alone rubbed off on me, and he didn't even know it.

Day six rolled around with a similar routine, and I still wondered if I could conquer this disease. My using thoughts hadn't gone away, and the guilt and shame of my past overwhelmed me into panic attacks. *Could I really change? Could I really be forgiven? Was absolution possible?* That was the ultimate question.

The Big Book's stories continued to narrate my lived experience, and I found comfort in every page. Why hadn't I read this years before? Why hadn't I sought out the answers? I had never been a reader before. Although my mom was always giving me books, I never once opened them—they just gathered dust at the top of the closet. If I had given them a shot earlier, would I be where I am? It didn't do good to dwell on what could've been, so I focused on what could be.

I deleted old numbers from my phone and changed my number. I didn't want the people from my past to contact me—not that they would—and I didn't want to remember their names. All of them were merely passers-by at the bar. They were probably still sitting in their favorite stools, bitching about the small things and only talking about themselves. They were people that I wasted so much time with, and I couldn't remember a single positive thing from all of those years. I wanted that wasted time and money back, but both were impossible.

Being in rehab is one of the most selfish but positive things you can do. It's a time to focus on yourself and no one else. It's a time to forgive the past and move forward. It's a time to rid of toxic people and a time to look inward. And it's one of the hardest things I would ever undertake.

Slowly but surely, I was starting to see the benefits of what I was doing. To anyone else, staying sober a few days may seem like a chump change, but to an addict, it feels like climbing the tallest mountain in the world.

So far, I had almost made it a week.

27

7 Days

It had been one week since I started rehab. I woke up that morning feeling content with where I was for the first time in a long while. Surprisingly, happiness could be found in other places besides the bottle. It came naturally through appreciating the simple things; the smell of a fresh cup of coffee, the warmth of a shower, the smell of freshly clean clothes, the sound of the morning news coming from the living room.

My night sweats stopped, which was a huge relief. I had run out of shirts to change into and was tired of the hot to cold flashes that plagued my sleep. Thoughts of drinking and using drugs were diminishing. *One day at a time*. I still struggled with ways to fill my time and any small chunks of free time scared me. *One day at a time*. It was also the fear of who I was just seven days ago that kept me straight.

Group therapy was working. It's funny how simply sharing your story and feelings works its way into breaking old habits. It happens almost subconsciously and without much effort. My counselors knew this but didn't say anything. It was their way of keeping me sober without telling me what to do. A few people I met on my first day were on their way out. They had completed their thirty-day stint and were being released back into the real world. They looked ready, which gave me hope that I might one day be too.

I'd take walks with my mom once she got home from work, and I described to her the whirlwinds of emotions I'd go in and out of. She, of course, was reading other people's testimonies online and shared a website where people described their experiences as they went through the days. Their descriptions were no different than what I was going through. Books gave her hope, and they were starting to give me hope as well. My brain was slowly starting to heal, and my body aches were going away. I made a physical appointment with my doctor to get my blood and liver checked. I was scared shitless after someone in my group described how their liver enzymes skyrocketed into dangerous levels. I knew mine would be high, but I needed evidence of it. It turns out my suspicions were right; my chart read in the high, high reds. It wasn't good news, but I needed a place to start in order to see progress.

Before, I thought God was something that was out of reach, something people used as an excuse for their behavior, either good or bad. Throughout my active addiction, I thought God gave up on me. He definitely didn't want to deal with someone like me. He had tried to reach out to me several times, but I threw it back in His face. I simply thought that my actions were unforgivable. Through my sobriety journey, I found this wasn't the case.

Addiction caused my life to become completely unmanageable and letting loose of the self-control I thought I had became a sticking point for the coming weeks. I had to release it to a higher power.

The thought of being sober forever sounded like an impossible feat. I wondered how I would have fun, if people would judge me for being a drug addict, if my brain could truly return to a normal state. I was scared I'd be doomed to my fate. But here I was, to my surprise, still sober on day seven. I was doing it. I could see my mom starting to have a sense of relief. She was glowing with happiness and no longer snapped awake in the middle of the night wondering if I was alive or not. My words were becoming actions, which were translating into real life change.

I was starting to develop a love of food, something I didn't know I had. During my addiction, the thought of eating was only to sustain my drinking and drug use. Above all, I didn't eat because it would ruin my buzz. If I did happen to eat an actual meal, which usually came on a Cookout tray, it would more than likely be thrown up in the toilet in the early morning hours. The sound of heaving and choking on my own vomit became an all-too familiar sound. It felt good to eat normally again. I was actually starting to fill in the gaps that my body ate away years before.

I began to set small, short-term goals. For example, making it to fourteen days sober was next on the list. My counselors told me that these goals were helpful, but the most important part was to not look too far ahead, or else the addiction would surely swallow me back up. I continually remembered what the old bearded guy in the lobby told me, "Just listen to your counselors and no one else."

The days felt long. I no longer had the juice to speed up time into a concept that was read by the rising and setting of the sun. Literally every minute had a purpose. Every minute was another reminder that I wasn't drinking. Every minute was another reminder that things were changing.

My previous actions couldn't be changed. But my actions moving forward were finally in my control. There were no more knee-jerk intoxicated decisions. No more putting my physical and mental health on the line. I had almost reached the most days sober I had been in over two years.

28

Then 2 Came

By the end of the second week, a few people from my original out-patient group fell off the wagon… or at least I assumed that after they didn't log on for two days in a row. It was a bit worrying, but it was their own lives and their own decisions. They entered the group with seemingly strong urges to get better, but as the days go by and addiction keeps knocking, it gets easier to forget the fervor with which you first entered.

One person talked about her boyfriend who was also an addict and attempting somewhat of a sober life with her. I thought that to be a recipe for disaster. I learned before that you couldn't get sober for anyone else but yourself. However, the boyfriend was still smoking weed, and she would be working behind the bar at an upcoming event.

I had been one of those people before and thought, *Well, I'll quit drinking, but I can still smoke weed* or *I can quit drinking and can still be around others who drink even if I'm only a few days in.* But the fact is smoking weed changes your mental state because it gets you high. You can't truly be sober if you still smoke weed; that's just not how it works. Getting sober isn't like going to the supermarket and picking and choosing what you like. It's a complete lifestyle change that some can't make.

The counselors were wary of people who thought they could be around others who drink so early in their sobriety. The fact is, one day, a sober person will have to be around people who drink. It's something you can't avoid, but it's something you can only deal with once your conviction is strong. You can't white knuckle the situation.

I think that's the saddest part about rehab and addiction in general—the realization that not everyone will make it through, that not everyone has the support system or the blocks in place to lift themselves up, that not everyone will give up control and relinquish it to their higher power. It's a realization that addiction is stronger than will power alone.

By this point, I still had thoughts of using; however, the urges were getting smaller. Physically getting out of bed was easier and the night sweats were no more. But the dreams did not cease. Dreams of drinking and using drugs were so vivid that I believed I had broken my sobriety once I woke up. Terrifying.

In addition to my group therapy, I attended Alcoholic Anonymous (AA) meetings online. I mostly just sat there and listened. I wasn't quite ready to share, but it helped to just be present. The meetings also had a wide range of people and time in sobriety—from those that were less than twenty-four hours in to people that had been sober for years. You could tell which people liked to boast about their time and take over the conversation. But you also had more humble people who were there to simply tell their lived experience and lend a hand.

An alcoholic's problems go far deeper than the drink itself. They may still lie, they may still cheat, and they may still spend their money on other vices like shopping. A sober person is still a human being, flawed to the core. Yes, the drink greatly affects a person's rational decision process. And yes, the drink does change a person's character. But there are far more things a drunk has to work on beyond the bottle. This is when faith comes into play. Faith was beginning to make me whole in other aspects of my life, and it was giving my integrity back.

Despite my qualms with some of the meeting attendees, it kept me in line with some sort of accountability. I found a sponsor after I heard him speak in a Thursday night meeting. He was a bald-headed guy with a thick country accent and almost fifteen years of sobriety from crack and alcohol under his belt. After hearing his story, I asked him to be my sponsor. I was nervous and totally uncomfortable with the idea of calling a stranger every day, but it was what my counselors told me to do. I followed through with it. Keeping my word and telling the truth became the foundational posts of the new person I wanted to be.

I'd give him the SparkNotes version of my story and how I ended up there. He then asked if this was something that I really wanted. The question really pissed me off. *Well, yes, why the hell was I there?! Why would I have asked you to be my sponsor if I didn't want to change?* However, I didn't think too much about it. I was in for the ride.

I was eager to jump through the chapters of the Big Book, but he took me through it at a snail's pace, going over one page a day. I questioned his ability to really help me through it. The thing is, there's no real road map to sobriety and everyone gets through it in their own way. There's no black and white answer. *One day at a time.* It was all I could hold on to.

With two and a half weeks down, I continued seeing the benefits of my sobriety and it amazed me just how fast my body was starting to heal. My poop was no longer icky yellow goo with spots of blood, my lower back was no longer sore, and I actually had energy to take walks. It felt good remembering falling asleep and waking up with a clean conscience. I had no one to apologize to or stories to weave to avoid harsh feedback or criticism.

We talked about giving ourselves, our will, to a higher power in the morning meetings and although I hadn't quite let go of it all, I was starting to understand what that meant. God wasn't there in some big overarching life-changing event. He was there in the small things—the small decisions, the small positive choices, and the small interactions with my family. I started to remember the subtle signs from the past. Back when I threw up in a church parking lot on the way back to Kinsley's apartment, or back when we were sitting in the field and I missed two shooting stars while looking down in the dark trying to find my drink, or when I woke up those many mornings with the self-awareness of knowing I had a problem but not following through with change. God had been trying to talk to me for so long, but it was impossible to see in active addiction. It had taken me years to get to this point, and I was finally starting to see how and why I had landed where I was. God had been there all along.

185

My thoughts of using drugs and alcohol were actually starting to go away— a miracle was happening. *How did my urge to drink disappear so fast? In only two and a half weeks? How?* I was relieved and excited by my progress, but I couldn't shake the impending feeling that things were going *too* well. My counselors told me that although it was awesome that I felt great and was starting to see the benefits, it was important to be aware that down days were inevitable. Sobriety would be a lifelong journey and the urge to use wouldn't magically go away forever. It was this awareness and alertness that kept me on my toes and kept me actively working at it. *One day at a time.* Each day would be another day to work on my sobriety. I needed to reel in my confidence and not get too far ahead of myself. I knew lulls in sobriety were inevitable, but I was starting to understand that a strong faith could weather any storm.

Sobriety is tough work and it got easier to see who was committed to change and who wasn't. I had been on both sides of the aisle before. For some, it was just a run through. Maybe someone had pushed them into the decision, but their heart wasn't in it. Some just hadn't scraped rock bottom enough. I saw myself and wanted to be there for them, but their journeys were out of my control. There were too many times to count where I walked through a counselor's door, an AA meeting, or dialed the phone number to a rehab facility with little intention of following through. It had literally taken me years to open up to the possibility.

One of the activities I was assigned was to list twenty things that were the result of my alcohol and drug use. I had never really paused to think about it, but when I did, it only took me about twenty minutes. It would have been easy to go all the way to a hundred. A few consequences I wrote included:

- Driving drunk almost every day
- Cheating on practically every girlfriend I had
- Stealing money from my parents
- Lying all the time
- Teaching kids while drunk

The exercise completely burst my ego. I was THE worst person I knew, and it sucked to share just how scummy I became. I finally slowed down long enough to see who I was, the damage I had caused and evaded. We shared our lists at the next session and others were equally as dark. I was in a group with people who lived in the shadows of addiction, but we were all slowly walking out of it. You could see the exhaustion in everyone's eyes but as they shared their lists, you could see the tension in their shoulders loosen and the clenching of their teeth release. Sharing was slowly easing the weight of the past.

I started seeing the world in a new light—God was here and around me. He had taken away my thoughts of drinking and using and started to allow me to sleep soundly at night. My God-skeptic ways crashed down around me, and it couldn't be explained by anything man-made. It was a miracle that I couldn't explain.

For those of you reading this who are not religious, I'm not here to convince you that there is a God or that you need to find Him yourself. All I'm saying is that in my experience, the change that was happening inside me didn't come from me. I had tried to use my human willpower to make changes before, but nothing happened except for dramatic failure.

Others around me had tried to break through to me and were stopped at the door. There was something much greater than me happening. It was really hard to understand then, and it is still hard to explain now. But as each day passed in the first month, the peace of mind I felt about the decisions I was making relaxed my soul. I couldn't reverse the past decisions that tore through people's lives like a hurricane, but I was starting to no longer live in the guilt and shame of the past. I started to see that moving forward was possible.

I bet you could ask thousands of other alcoholics and they would tell a similar tale. We are selfish and hard-headed by nature and believe two truths: one, our world view is the right one and two, we are in control of our lives. The sad reality is that we have zero control. The bottle or whatever the drug of choice is becomes our god, and it doesn't give a shit about anything else.

Ridding myself of the shame and guilt was one of the hardest things to accept. I often didn't feel like I was worthy of that forgiveness. My counselors repeatedly told me that forgiveness was the first crucial step to moving forward. It was something I had to accept. I had to accept that the person I was during active addiction was me, but I could choose to be a better person, the person I was always supposed to be. It felt like the weathered skin of that young, stupid teenager that left for college was being shed. I knew God had already forgiven me, and the next step was forgiving myself.

I was attending AA meetings regularly and called my sponsor both on the good and the bad days. It was a bit monotonous doing so and most of the time, I called him with nothing to say. It was awkward, but I was only following the playbook laid out for me. In many respects, I felt as though he wasn't reaching out enough, and eventually I lost contact with him after I forgot to call him one day. I guess he thought I wasn't hungry enough. It hurt, but he was a stranger who was offering himself for free. Why should he care about me? Maybe he fell off the wagon?

As I approached day twenty-eight, my body was starting to feel the best it ever had. It had rid itself of all the toxins and drugs for the first time ever. I no longer was impatient or short with my parents and took the time to sit down and have conversations that were longer than two minutes. I became interested in others around me—what their days were like, their goals, what struggles they were going through, and their opinions.

My destruction had branched into every life that came close to me. My addiction had been killing my mom, and it was now clear that it caused tension in their marriage. My addiction had become more than my own, and I felt immense guilt and shame for what I had done.

Substances do a weird thing to a person's psyche. It becomes the only thing you think about in the morning and the last thing you think about at night. It becomes your purveyor and your master. And you become strangely okay with everything. It takes everything you love and doesn't ask for permission.

I was approaching my thirty-day mark, a big milestone in the mind of a recovering addict. It felt like the longest month I ever endured. It was amazing to simply remember the day. There were no blurry nights and heavy mornings. There were no regrets or empty promises. There were no half-hearted hugs or kisses, no spine-killing back aches. I followed through on my words and proved to myself that although I only had a short amount of sobriety time, I was capable of change. I showed myself that the person I used to be wasn't who I had to be. I was becoming the person God made me to be all along. I just had to be sober for one more day to continue on that path.

29

Learning to Live Beyond

I write this last chapter with almost a year and a half of sobriety under my belt. It may not sound like a lot, but it's a lot to me. I drank and did drugs practically every day for eleven years, looking at myself in the mirror and crumbling under the shadows of addiction. Like most addicts, the process of sinking deeper into addiction was slow and steady. It wasn't an overnight switch; it was a gradual simmer that eventually boiled over.

I still have no idea how I didn't kill someone while driving drunk thousands of times, how I'm currently not sitting in jail or lying in an early grave. I have no idea how my brain is still intact, and my body is still healthy. I can only equate this to pure luck and the power of prayers of family and even strangers. But luck could only last so long. I was, without a doubt, running out of chances.

I used people, played with girlfriends, stole, lied, and was a selfish prick almost every day of my life. I'm not here to make excuses and tell you that my addiction was the culprit in me acting the way I did. The person that did all of those cruel things was me. I clearly had—and still have—problems outside of drinking and using drugs that need to be resolved and talked through. I think for outsiders it's easy to ask, "Why didn't you just stop?" That's a valid question. However, during active addiction, an addict gives up a lot of free will to make their own decisions because, well, the person they actually are isn't consciously making decisions—the drug or drink is.

I want to drive home the point that any addict is capable of being saved from this way of life… but that change can only come from themselves. This is a hard realization for outsiders to come to terms with. Loved ones want to save that person. They want to push them into rehab and therapy. They want to take away their wallets and hide their booze. They want to move to different cities and go to church. And they want to change their own lifestyles in hopes that the addict may follow. But the fact is, most addicts will have to scrape bottom many times before they themselves want to seek help.

Although my story may seem crazy or unique to me, most recovered addicts will say this isn't far from their own experiences. We addicts have more in common than not.

An active addict will be the first to say their truth is unique, that no one will understand them or that they have it all figured out. They will say they don't need friends or family to help them, that their professional life isn't suffering. An addict will push away everything around them besides their vice. The irony is that what's killing them is exactly what they want more of.

The sad reality of it all is that not everyone will get over their disease. Many will have an early death and take it to their grave. Some don't have the support like I did, the resources to attend a rehab program or talk to a psychiatrist and therapist. Some don't have a roof over their head and are battling poverty and addiction at the same time. I couldn't imagine that.

I jumped from job to job and place to place, constantly thinking that changing a location would change me. But chaos followed me wherever I went. It wasn't the place that was the problem, it was me. I'm sure I ran across countless good people that would've been great friends at the time. However, no one was better than the substances.

I personally could not have gotten over my own struggles without the help of a loving family, so I can only imagine how hard it would be on your own. Addiction knows no boundaries. It doesn't matter the color of your skin or the amount of money in your bank account. It doesn't matter how well you were raised or how smart you may think you are. Addiction will creep its way into the lives of anyone. It's a slow process that compounds on its own and usually takes years to show its full ugly face.

Addiction will always be around, and so will drugs and alcohol. Alcohol is literally everywhere in society; you simply can't escape it. I'm not here to tell you that no one should drink. Many people can drink normally, and most will never face this terrible disease. But I know that a lot of people struggle with it and never address it. Some say, "Well, I don't drink every day," or "Drinking has never gotten in the way of my family life or my job." If one truly has a problem, the small signs will be there. They'll hide alcohol in unassuming cups; they'll drink earlier and earlier in the day; they'll buy more liquor when the cabinet is already full; and activities, no matter what it is, will have to involve alcohol.

Addiction is a quiet disease that has wound its tentacles deep into the fabric of society. It's a disease that isolates its host and thrives off of silence. As an addict, I wish I addressed just how bad my addiction was earlier in my life. My rock bottom was a series of rock bottoms, which is usually the case for most addicts. I didn't seek help until everything in my life came to a head.

I've treated people like shit, and I've ruined a lot of relationships. I can never take back those actions. I still live with the guilt from what I've done, but I have shown through my actions that I am capable of change. It's *that* realization that gives me strength. It's the realization that I *can choose* not to be that person. Now that I'm sober and can think clearly, I *can choose* not to drink and use drugs. I *can choose* a sober life.

Although I'm still early in this process, I have a newfound strength, both within myself and spiritually. I have found a peace of mind in the person I am today. However, I am also painfully aware that not everyone close to me has healed. My addiction caused destruction in the lives of everyone that I came across, and me simply being sober won't heal or speed up that process within others. Healing happens slowly and it happens in making the right decisions every day. I thank God that I didn't completely destroy everything for good, but I know that what I've done has lasting effects.

I still have my health; I still have my hope; and I still have my family. I know I've put them through hell. I know that they all had sleepless nights, endless nightmares, and crippling anxiety. I know that they are fearful of me relapsing. But I have no intentions of ever going back. I must stay vigilant. I must actively do things every day in my sobriety. I have found a new me, or maybe I just returned back to the person I left long ago. I hope that you find peace and hope in my own story, and that this memoir has helped you better understand the madness that surrounds an active addict's behavior and ways of thinking. If someone you know is caught in the shadows, don't give up. Deep down, they are still there. Deep down, they are tired of being pretty quiet.

193

Epilogue
A father's perspective

Reading *Pretty Quiet* was a gut-wrenching, heart-sinking experience that brought second thoughts and many regrets on how I handled fatherhood for David. The authentic and real-time stories David tells in the book brought to reality the depth and severity of David's drug and alcohol issues of the last eleven years. I knew David was smoking pot and drinking in his early twenties, but I never realized the partying penetrated to the depths of his soul and almost killed him. His habits not only included pot and alcohol, but over time heroin, cocaine, ecstasy, pills and meth entered his daily routine. My biggest fear as he was going in and out of denial was that he may take his own life to escape the harsh grip the drugs and alcohol had on his life. That fear was brought to reality in his book when he mentioned he thought about buying a gun and taking his life. David went through hell for 11 years battling the rollercoaster ride of alcoholism and addiction. This destructive ride started when he left for college.

David was a sweet, "pretty quiet," kind child who loved his older brother Drew and adored his baby sister Mattie. In high school, he was a kid who enjoyed making movies and making art. I think his talent came from my Uncle Bill who was a talented artist. David was a decent athlete who played Varsity sports, probably to please me, and to show his older brother Drew he could also play multiple sports at high level competition. David benefited from my experience coaching his brother Drew, as I pulled back from the yelling and overanalyzing each play of the game and overemphasizing the importance and meaning of the sport. I tried to encourage him in whatever made him happy. I always told him to find a passion and pursue it with hard work and determination. Art and making movies were his high school passions. While I missed him playing sports, I realized I needed to support whatever made him happy, so I did everything I could to support his love of art.

My goal as his father was to provide a loving family environment that provided unconditional love and support, while disciplining, teaching and correcting when needed. I think I did most of those, but I do reflect on decisions I made and situations I put David in that may have contributed to his harmful habits. I look back at my parenting and would make many changes.

I had a suspicion that he was stealing money and pills from me, but I never really tackled the issue other than to ask him. He would respond quickly with a "No, I can't believe you would accuse me of that." Deep inside I knew he was doing it, but I let it slide time after time. I should have applied consequences and retribution.

I also look back when my children were in middle and high school, and I had way too many parties at our house where alcohol was flowing to the point of overindulgence. Children observe what parents do and say, and they have a natural tendency to follow in their footsteps. As David notes in his book, there were occasions when I partied with David and supplied the toxins that eventually started his abuse. I think I wanted to add "friend" to the label of "son," and this fueled my indiscretions. I found it hard to separate the two sometimes.

As I read through the book with eyes wide open, my heart and soul tearing at the seams and tears flowing down my cheeks, I am thankful David hit rock bottom and realized that if he did not change, he would soon die. David was the only one who could change his situation. His mother and I did everything we could to lift him up and encourage him to get help. We provided shelter and food when David would hit bottom, but we did not realize he was consuming excessive drugs and alcohol while under our roof. Managing a child's addictions can be taxing on marriages as Martha and I realized when she would have one approach and I would have another.

David's body and soul were shredded and ravished with abuse that needed repair. Relationships, parents, and siblings could not do what was needed to fix the problem. David went to a higher power and found faith and hope in God's love and forgiveness. I am thankful for the counselors and staff at Cumberland Heights Rehabilitation Center, and for AA groups in the Nashville area that genuinely and lovingly supported David to the point where he could see daylight and hope in the future. David completed a 30 day out-patient program at Cumberland Heights that changed his life. David has been 18 months clean and knows it is a daily battle. David's shame and guilt has been washed away through professional help and the support and love of family and friends. But, most importantly, David has come to the realization that the higher power of God's grace and mercy has lifted him to a position of strength and perseverance. David knows his family has forgiven him and wants him to thrive in this new sober adventure he is currently pursuing with determination and grit.

I think David and I share a lot of common mistakes (the apple did not fall far from the tree), and he has helped me realize the importance of self-control and family. I hope David will forgive me for my bad parenting decisions and know he has my unconditional love and support in his new adventure and zest for life.

David is currently a straight "A" student at Grand Canyon University seeking his master's degree in alcohol and drug abuse counseling. I can't think of anyone else who would qualify more for such a career. I know he views this as a way to give back to those in need of recovery and support.

If you are currently dealing with a child suffering from and battling drug and/or alcohol abuse, **Don't Give Up On Them**. Provide support that does not enable. Provide love that is grounded in faith, and pray they come to the realization that they need professional counseling. The only way out is when they want out and seek professional help. Take each day at a time, and know this dreaded disease can be whipped and destroyed.

May God be your support and anchor!

A Letter to Brothers

I bet this is a place you never thought you or your family would be. We all grew up hearing the special guest speakers at school, and I think most people just scoff and think how that won't happen to them or their family. Well, it does – and when you are watching someone you love fall into a bottomless pit of darkness, the emotions of fear, anger, love, hopelessness, and hope are all ones you will battle with daily. These are all emotions you will need to express at different times, not only to help your brother or sister, but to help yourself as well. This journey will have more lows than highs, and one that is going to put your family relationships to the test. Below are some main points that come to me when I look back at the journey my family has been on.

Don't Question the Past

All siblings have a past filled with good times, bad times, and everything in between. Don't look back and question when you could have done something differently or been more present. Dwelling on these thoughts will eat at you and make you believe you are a reason why your sibling has gone down this path. The fact of the matter is this isn't about you, and your past relationship isn't the reason your brother or sister is here in the present.

Push for Love

There are going to be instances in which you feel angry, sad, and like all hope is lost. Try not to let these emotions overtake you, and instead, push for love. Let that love you feel for your brother or sister overshadow these other emotions, because love is the main thing your sibling needs. It may need to be tough love at times, but pushing that love forward will help when their feelings are the darkest.

Take the Bad with the Good

There are going to be good days, but more than likely, the bad days will outweigh the good. Days when you will wait by the phone waiting to hear from your brother or a family member to get the latest updates and praying it won't be a call telling you the worst has happened. On those bad days, it is going to seem like all hope is lost. You will think your brother or sister just doesn't want help, and you will believe s/he prefers this lifestyle. When these days happen, take a few moments to try and find something good on that day. As small as it may be, finding at least one thing to be thankful for each day will give you that hope and strength to continue to be there for your sibling when the next bad day comes.

Do Not Resent Family

Everyone is going to have different views on what is best for your brother or sister. Your parents, siblings, and friends may all have a different idea on the best way to help. Try not to resent them if it is not what you think is best. Try not to get angry if you feel like your parents are being too "easy" or enabling him or her. Parents have the hardest job in this journey, trying to navigate helping their child while also not enabling their bad decisions. It is a parental duty I hope I never have to experience. I can't express how much respect I have for my parents as I look back at how they handled the situation. Yet at times, when we were in the thick of it, I experienced feelings of anger and resentment that my parents were being too easy and not putting their foot down firmly enough. Experiencing these emotions is normal, but remember that s/he is their child who is going through this, and they are on the front lines fighting the best they know how. Now, I'm not saying you should not express your feelings to them and share what you think the best course of action may be, but it is important to support what they choose. Family sticking together and being a united front is something I really attribute to saving my brother.

This journey was tough for our whole family. It tested each of us in different ways, but none more than my brother. I am so thankful for how close my brother and I have gotten during this journey, and I will continue to fight by his side daily. My brother, even though he is younger, is someone I look up to and have so much respect for. As I'm sure you have seen through this book, this is a battle that only the strong will win. I can say without a doubt my brother is one of the strongest men I know. It is a battle my brother and your sibling will fight the rest of their lives. But you can give your brother or sister the greatest weapon, unconditional love.

Drew Newson

A Letter to Sisters

Being the daughter, the sister who doesn't have the addiction, places an undeserved angelic aura around you. As the baby of the family, everyone wants to protect you from anything that could taint your innocence. "Everything is fine," "Don't worry about it," "David is just going through a tough time right now." Hearing your parents whisper in the kitchen hoping you're not paying any attention from the living room. Loud phone calls happening in the master bedroom. The "baby" knows something is going on. Yet you're placed behind a curtain– all hoping that if you don't see it, don't directly interact with it, then your fragile emotional state will remain intact; your innocence will remain pure. It's painful. Sensing and feeling the tension, the heartache, the secrets, but not being told any truth directly.

Maybe I would have been told if I had asked. I think there was a part of me as a young girl and teenager that didn't want to know the truth; that knowledge would fracture my family in some way. As I went to college, graduated, started my career, I did start to ask more directly; however, the people I asked were everyone but David. Calling and texting Mom, Dad, and Drew became my news lines. "What's going on with David?", "Why is he doing this?", "I'm so worried about him." Then the non-David person on the other line would respond with their most recent update and opinion on David's decisions and condition. It was not until things got so blatantly and so dangerously bad did I begin to communicate with David directly.

David was my closest friend growing up. He would always let me tag-along no matter if he was alone or with his friends. Building forts, playing kickball or jackpot in the cul-de-sac, biking on the greenway to get some candy at the gas station were some of our favorite activities together. I knew Drew loved me, but our 7 year age gap felt enormous as children. David was kind, understanding, creative, and adventurous. His strengths were not my own, and I loved seeing the world through his eyes. It was terrifying just thinking that the brother I so admired and was so close to could possibly be an addict. Didn't those people have missing teeth, broken families, and live on the street? My brother, who had the same childhood and opportunities as me, could not possibly be an addict.

When I gripped the truth and the gravity of that truth, I could finally be direct with my brother. It's a swirl of emotion having a loved one struggle with addiction. I was so angry at David for putting our family through all of this pain and frustration– even more so placing my parents through that pain. I wanted my parents to cut all ties at one point– stop enabling his addictive behavior; maybe when he sees what it's like on the street alone then that will sober him up real fast. Reflecting, maybe I did think I sat on a heavenly throne… I was frustrated at David for taking so long to realize and to admit he had a problem. When he quickly left the in-patient rehab facility my elation that this was his turning point plummeted. It seemed like he had given up. In typical David fashion, however, he had to do it his way, and in-patient was not best for *his* recovery journey. I was proud of David for each day of his first year of sobriety. An accomplishment that represented the homecoming of the prodigal son.

David and I have talked more in the past year and a half than we have in the past decade. In the beginning, there were a lot of phone calls and texts centered upon his recovery– checking in on how he was doing, talking about his group support sessions, if he was still having cravings for alcohol. Now the conversations are about his master's degree classes, how his garden is growing, making fun of how he wants to live remotely in the mountains, and updating him on how my volleyball team is doing. We have a genuine relationship because he is genuinely himself now.

I still have fears that David will relapse and the cycle will start again but this time he wouldn't make it out like he has in the past. However, through my faith, I am comforted in the peace that

David is healing. He has a renewed relationship with Christ and is finally excited about his future path of counseling others who are lost in the throes of addiction. Our family is healing alongside him, but I, we, celebrate each day that David is alive and doing so much better.

So sisters, be there for your loved one and when you get tired of being kept behind the curtain, step through the center instead of on the wing. Show your love for your brother by being honest about your hurt and disappointment but also show your love for his steps in the better direction. Have faith in *Him* and have faith in *him*.

Mattie Newson

Acknowledgements

My thoughts and prayers are with those still in the thick of addiction. May you find hope in the darkness and strength in the lows. You are never alone. Find love, find community, and know that you can beat addiction.

I want to thank my mom, my sister, and my editor for helping me with getting this memoir ready for publication.

Pretty Quiet

David Newson

Made in United States
Orlando, FL
11 January 2024

42378284R00114